THE AVEl . ._.. . .

OF THE

APOSTLES & PROPHETS

Workbook

By
Arthur M. Ogden

Printed in the United States of America

Second Edition, 2001

Third Edition, 2013

ISBN 10: 0-9646497-2-1
ISBN 13: 978-0-9646497-2-9

Questions and scripture quotations are based on the *King James Version* of the Bible, unless otherwise noted.

OGDEN PUBLICATIONS

Aogden.com • ogdenpub@aogden.com

Lesson 1

General Observations

Compared to other books of the Bible, the book of Revelation is the most difficult to comprehend and confusing to study. It is the most misunderstood, misapplied, speculated upon and talked about of all Bible books. Yet, it is the most beautiful in thought, challenging in nature, comprehensive in scope, prophetic in design and comforting in purpose of all the books of the Bible.

It is a masterpiece in literature. It challenges: (a) our intellects, i.e., our abilities to reason, judge, comprehend, and understand; (b) our imagination, i.e., our ability to formulate images or ideas corresponding to those revealed; (c) our knowledge and understanding of **the truth** revealed in our Bibles; (d) our will to learn; (e) our patience and (f) our endurance. The Revelation unites Old Testament prophecies of victory and desolation with similar New Testament prophecies and shows them as impending historical events **shortly to come to pass.** History shows their fulfillment.

This book breathes a message directly from the throne of God of His faithfulness to avenge Himself and His people of their enemies giving comfort and consolation to those oppressed.

What Is The Book of Revelation?

The book of Revelation is often called "The Apocalypse." This is because the first word of the book in the Greek language is *apokalupsis* and translated in our versions as *"the revelation."* The word means "an uncovering, or unveiling" and is used about a dozen times in the New Testament. Related words are used another 30 times. The Revelation is an uncovering, or unveiling, of historical events **"shortly to come to pass"** (1:1). The Apocalypse contains **past, present,** and **future** events (1:19). Some of the events foretold were expected immediately while some have not been fulfilled to this day.

The book of Revelation is a book of warning and comfort. It warned five of the seven churches to repent, and it warned those who had the **mark of the beast** of coming wrath (14:9-11). Indeed, all of the wicked of the earth are warned (21:8). On the other hand the saints are promised blessings abundantly if they keep God's commandments, overcome and remain faithful to death. What a joy to be numbered among the saints. Surely, *"the sufferings of this present time are not worthy to be compared with the glory which shall be revealed in us"* (Rom.8:18).

The Unique Features of the Book

Revelation stands alone in New Testament literature. Of the 27 New Testament books, four are about the life of Christ, one about the beginning and spread of Christianity, twenty-one are about Christian living, and one is a prophecy of impending historical events. All scripture is inspired of God (2 Tim.3:16-17; 2 Pet.1:20-21), however, the book of Revelation stands alone because it was **signified** unto John by **the angel** of the Lord (1:1).

The book of Revelation teaches nothing new. The doctrine by which we are to live and overcome was revealed by the Holy Spirit in the other New Testament books and is reflected in the statement, *"He that hath an ear, let him hear what the Spirit saith unto the churches"* (2:7,11,17,29; 3:6,13,22).

The **Apocalypse** is the last book of the Bible. It was placed there by man. No other place could be more fitting because this book recognizes the teaching of the Bible as the Spirit revealed word of God, the source of all revealed spiritual truth. As a prophecy, it foretold historical events to be fulfilled immediately upon its revelation. The fulfillment of those prophecies gave divine approval and sanction to all the books of the Bible.

The Author of the Book

The book of Revelation was written by John (1:1,4,9; 21:2; 22:8). He was a servant of Christ (1:1), a *"brother, and companion in tribulation, and in the kingdom and patience of Jesus Christ."* John was on the Isle of *"Patmos, for the word of God, and for the testimony of Jesus Christ"* (1:9). Further identification was not given. Many early church fathers attributed the book to the apostle John. Similarities in characteristics seem to indicate that the Apocalypse, the Gospel of John, and the Epistles of John were written by the same person whose name we know only as John. The nature of the book demands the essence of a man who compares in abilities to a fully inspired Peter or Paul. No other John, except the apostle, measures up to their image. In fact, he must be able to stand beside an Isaiah, Jeremiah, Ezekiel or Zechariah, for the **Apocalypse** encompasses the fullness of these prophets and more.

No other John we know measures up to the likeness of these notable ones.

Conclusion

In review, we have learned that the book of Revelation is a masterpiece presentation. No other book in our Bible compares with it. Historical events were revealed to take place **shortly** after the book was written which, when fulfilled, placed God's stamp of approval upon it and the rest of the Bible.
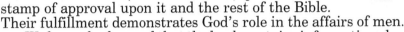
Their fulfillment demonstrates God's role in the affairs of men.

We have also learned that the book contains information about events of the past, present and future (1:19). This establishes a very important feature in our attempts to unravel its message. We must distinguish between these events and, when we do, we will have established a chronological order in our studies. **If chronological order is present, we must recognize it.**

Home Exercise

Our home exercises for the introductory section of this study are designed to encourage the reading of the book of Revelation. The more you know about the book, the more you will learn. Please read the book.

Locate Chapter(s) in Revelation Where Topics Are Found

1. 144,000	Ch._____	12. Red horse	Ch._____
2. 666	Ch._____	13. Babylon	Ch._____
3. 1260 days	Ch._____	14. 6 winged beings	Ch._____
4. Philadelphia	Ch._____	15. Satan is bound	Ch._____
5. A bird cage	Ch._____	16. Patmos	Ch._____
6. Lamb appears	Ch._____	17. Red Dragon	Ch._____
7. Song of Moses	Ch._____	18. Tree of Life	Ch._____
8. Nicolaitans	Ch._____	19. Little book	Ch._____
9. Lamb's wife	Ch._____	20. Wormwood	Ch._____
10. King of Kings	Ch._____	21. Armageddon	Ch._____
11. Abaddon	Ch._____	22. The winepress	Ch._____

MULTIPLE-CHOICE: (Most answers are found in Rev.1:1-3)

1. The book of Revelation is sometimes called (the synoptic gospel; the apocalypse; Armageddon).

2. The book of Revelation is (an epistle; a history; a prophecy).

3. Read Revelation 1:1,19; 22:6 and decide whether the book is about (past, present and future things; only things shortly to come to pass; only about things thousands of years ahead).

4. The book of Revelation was written by (John Mark; John the Baptist; John).

5. The book is said to have been revealed by (the Holy Spirit; an angel; a dream).

6. The message is said to be given first by God to (John; the angel; Jesus Christ).

7. The message was (spoken; signified; visualized) to John.

8. The person who studies the book of Revelation is said to be (cursed; stupid; blessed).

9. The time for the prophecy of the book to be fulfilled was (a long way off; at hand; doubtful).

Lesson 2

"Blessed is he that readeth, and they that hear the words of this prophecy, and keep those things which are written therein: for the time is at hand" (Rev.1:3).

You Can Understand This Book

Often our minds are closed to a study of the book of Revelation. We have heard so many negative things about the book that we are afraid to study it. We feel the book is too difficult for us. The author of the book thought differently, however, because he promised **blessedness** to those who read and study the book of Revelation. Should we not give this inspired apostle the benefit of doubt and see if indeed his promise is true?

It is plain, from the first verse of the book (1:1), that this book contains a message directly from the throne of God. Later chapters (4 & 5) also emphasize this point. Does it seem reasonable God would reveal to His servants **things which must shortly come to pass** without giving any clue what those things were? Would God reveal a book, instructing us to read and comprehend it, if it were impossible to be understood? I believe God has given everything needed to unravel the mysteries of this book and, when we have been successful, we will enjoy the **blessedness** of which John spoke.

The Language of the Book

We are introduced to the kind of language employed in the book in Revelation 1:1 (cf.15:1). God's message was **signified** to John by the angel of Jesus Christ. To signify something is to **sign-i-fy** or **symbolize** it. This means we are given important and helpful information by signs or symbols. We are familiar with **sign** language. We use signs every day, and we understand them. Signs are not the literal things which they signify but the things signified are literal. If, while driving down the road, we see a sign with an arrow curved to the left, we understand we are approaching a curve in the road bearing to the left. The sign is not the curve but it tells us a literal curve lies ahead and we should use caution.

Sign (symbolic) language is abundant in the book of Revelation. This language was designed to uncover the literal events **which were shortly to come to pass.** Making the wrong decision about the meaning of this language will affect our conclusions.

One guideline we must adopt from the beginning is: **we will always accept John's explanation of the meaning of a sign without question.** This is important because John gives at least three dozen identifications of signs used in the book. For example: the seven stars in the right hand of the vision personage symbolize the angels of the seven churches. The seven golden candlesticks symbolize the seven churches (1:20). No doubt John revealed these identifications to assist in our comprehension of the message. I suggest that any interpretation placed upon any part of the book of Revelation that cannot accept John's identification cannot be a correct interpretation of the Apocalypse. So, in our studies, let us always look for John's explanations.

"This book speaks not the language of Paul, but the Old Testament prophets Isaiah, Ezekiel, and Daniel."[1] Their writings portray God's dealing with the nations, particularly with Israel, Judah and Jerusalem. It should be noted that Revelation compares in language to the writings of these Old Testament prophets.

"The Book of Revelation is the most thoroughly Jewish in its language and imagery of any New Testament book."[2] The signs, symbols, types and language are Jewish. The use of the beasts, harps, vials, horses, winds, angels, trumpets, candlesticks, censers, incense, pit, lamb, altar, temple, and twelve tribes, are Jewish. The book is completely saturated with Jewish thought, expression and symbology. All of this argues for a Jewish understanding and application for the book.

Methods of Interpretation

There are many approaches to the study of the book of Revelation. Listed below are five of the most popular approaches to a study of the book.

The Futurist View: This method of interpretation sees the book as yet unfulfilled. Millennialist and dispensationalist hold to this view which is the most popular view among denominationalist today. This view places literal interpretations upon many of the signs and symbols of the book. Historical events are projected for future fulfillment in a 1000 year literal reign of Christ on earth.

---

[1] Jenkins, Ferrell, *The Old Testament In The Book of Revelation.* (Cogdill Foundation Publications, 1972, page 22).

[2] *Ibid.*, page 22.

This interpretation would have been meaningless to the people of John's day.

The Preterist View: This method of interpretation sees the book being fulfilled during the lives of the people addressed. Unfortunately, this forces them to interpret all of the language of the book to the first century.

The Early Historical View: The book is pictured as written to the people of John's day and fulfilled for the most part in the first two centuries. The view seeks to derive a message applicable for all times.

The Continuous Historical View: This approach presents the book as a forecast of the church with the rise of the papacy, Mohammedanism, the reformation, etc. Modern world leaders are often imagined as foreseen by John. This view would have been meaningless to the people John addressed.

The Spiritual View: This position says that the things revealed were not actual events, but were symbolic of spiritual and temporal forces working in the world in which, ultimately, the spiritual are victorious. This view opens the door to every interpretation imaginable.

Our view of the book of Revelation should not be molded by the theories of men but by the word of God. The book must be understood as meaningful to the people John addressed and it must be understood as historical.

Home Exercise

Read The Questions Before Reading "Revelation"

1. List the various things in the book said to have horns:

   _____, _____, _____, _____,
   _____, _____.

2. List those things of which it is said there was **SEVEN,** and indicate the number of times each is found:

   _____#__, _____#__, _____#__, _____#__,
   _____#__, _____#__, _____#__, _____#__,
   _____#__, _____#__, _____#__, _____#__,
   _____#__, _____#__, _____#__, _____#__,
   _____#__, _____#__, _____#__, _____#__.

   TOTAL NUMBER OF TIMES USED: _____.

3. List those things of which it is said there were **TWELVE:**

   _____, _____, _____, _____,
   _____, _____, _____, _____,
   _____.

4. List those things of which it is said there were **FOUR:**

   _____, _____, _____, _____,
   _____, _____.

TRUE OR FALSE:

1._____ The book of Revelation was revealed to John by the Holy Spirit.

2._____ The message was **signified** to John.

3._____ John said everyone must read the book to profit from it.

4._____ We may use **sign** and **symbol** interchangeably.

5._____ No one questions the apostle John's authorship.

6._____ John often explains the meaning of signs used.

7._____ We should accept his explanation only if it supports our interpretation of the Apocalypse.

8._____ Revelation reveals by symbolic language historical events before they happened.

9._____ These events should have chronological order.

10._____ The book of Revelation does not need to be harmonized with the rest of the Bible.

Lesson 3

Dating the Book of Revelation

Establishing the date of Bible books is helpful in understanding their message. Knowing where and when the author wrote helps us imagine the setting with all of its attendant surroundings, and helps us comprehend more fully the message of each book.

The Apocalypse is unique in that the date of its composition affects the interpretation placed upon its message. It is clear that the book purports to reveal **things which were shortly to come to pass.** The proximity of the events to the time of writing is evident. The time of John's writing was shortly before the fulfilling of the events foretold.

There are two general views. The first argues that the book portrays the desolation of the nation of Israel and the destruction of Jerusalem. This demands that the book be written shortly before those things occurred in 70 A.D. during the reign of Roman Emperor, **Nero** (54-68 A.D.). We call this view **the early date.** The second view argues that the book portrays the developing conflict between Christians and the Roman Empire. This would demand that the book be written shortly before that conflict occurred, around 95 or 96 A.D., during the reign of Emperor **Domitian** (81-96 A.D.). We call this view **the late date.**

The Evidence

In drawing a conclusion as to when the Apocalypse was written, we consider the **internal** (within the book) and **external** (outside the book) evidence. The strongest evidence for **the early date** is internal. The strongest evidence for **the late date** is external. Space will not permit a discussion of all evidence here.

Evidence for the Early Date

While there are dozens of arguments that could be made for the early date, our space limits us to only two.[3] (1) According to many prominent authorities, the number of the beast identified

---

[3] Gentry, Kenneth L., Jr., *Before Jerusalem Fell*, (Institute for Christian Economics, 1989). This extensive work of more than 350 pages on dating the Book of Revelation is a must in studying the date of the Apocalypse.

Nero Caesar.[4] The number is 666, and **Neron Caesar** (his name correctly spelled) computes to the magic number. If we drop the **n**, as usual, the number adds to only 616, the precise number, according to Irenaeus (175 A.D.), appearing in many early manuscripts of the Apocalypse. Since the sea beast symbolizes the Roman Empire and Emperor Nero was the first to **make war on New Testament saints** (cf.Rev.13:7), this identification fits perfectly with the picture being developed.

(2) John identified a specific time period in 17:9-11. Seven kings are mentioned; *"five are fallen, and one is, and the other is not yet come."* These kings were associated with the seven headed scarlet beast identified as the Roman Empire. Josephus, the noted Jewish historian, numbers the Roman emperors so that we need not make a mistake in our count. He identifies Augustus, Tiberius and Caligula as the second, third and fourth emperors.[5] Accordingly, Julius, whose family name, **Caesar**, became the official title for all the Emperors, was the first king. Claudius was the fifth and **Nero** the sixth. In this lesson, our interest is only in the one who **"is,"** the sixth who was **Nero**. This establishes Nero as the ruling king at the time John saw the vision.

Evidence for the Late Date

Those contending for **the late date** depend heavily upon a statement by Irenaeus (130-200 A.D.), who is said was a pupil of Polycarp who, in turn, was a pupil of John. He spoke of "him who saw the Apocalypse" saying, "For it was not a great while ago that (it or he) was seen, but almost in our own generation, toward the end of Domitian's reign." To many this statement, though written nearly 100 years after Domitian's reign, settles the question.

Those who argue the late date also contend that, since Revelation deals with emperor worship and wide-spread persecution, the book had to be written late, probably late in Domitian's reign (95-96 A.D.). Neither argument is strong enough to build a case upon, however, for two reasons. First, because emperor worship existed for over 100 years before Domitian's reign[6] and, second, there is little evidence, if any, of the Romans persecuting Christians during his reign.[7]

In our opinion the evidence for **the late date** is weak. While we believe emperor worship and persecutions are in evidence in the

---

[4] Jenkins, Ferrell, *Studies in the Book of Revelation*, 4th Printing, Rev. 6-14-83, page 22.

[5] Josephus, *Antiquities of the Jews*, 18,2,2; 16,6,2.

[6] Jenkins, Ferrell, *Emperor Worship in the Book of Revelation*, 1988.

[7] Ogden, Arthur M., & Jenkins, Ferrell, *Did Domitian Persecute Christians?* An exchange carried in Searching the Scriptures, 1989. Available on the Internet in Adobe Acrobat format at **http://www.aogden.com**.

book of Revelation, we do not believe this is the primary subject matter.

The Primary Subject

It is evident in Revelation that God's wrath was directed toward someone involved in persecuting God's people. Who are they? Establishing who they are will solve many problems.

Here it would be helpful to understand the four natural divisions of the book of Revelation. (1) The Seven Churches of Asia, chapters 1-3. (2) The Heavenly Apocalypse, chapters 4-11. (So called because God's heavenly throne is established and His wrath poured out as ordered and directed by that throne.) (3) The Earthly Apocalypse, chapters 12-20. (So called because the earthly instruments, used by God to carry out His wrath, are viewed.) (4) The new Jerusalem, chapters 21-22.

The clues to the understanding of the subject matter revealed in Revelation are found in the two middle sections, chapters 4-20. These clues may be divided into two parts: (1) those which reveal the primary and (2) secondary subject matter. Study the following passages in the Apocalypse which establish the primary subject under consideration.

The Vengeance of Revelation

6:9-11 This text reveals the opening of the fifth seal depicting martyred saints crying for vengeance. They were given white robes and told to rest a little season until others of their brethren were also killed. Careful study will **demand** we identify these martyrs as Old Testament saints who died for the word of God.

11:17-18 This text is a part of the rejoicing taking place in heaven following the destruction of a city identified as the place *"where our Lord was crucified"* (11:8). Note: Reward was given to God's *"servants the **prophets**"* in this outpouring of wrath.

16:5-6 We are now in the third division of the book and someone is judged worthy of God's wrath being poured upon them because they *"shed the blood of saints and **prophets**."*

17:6 Babylon the Great is pictured as *"drunken with the blood of the saints, and with the blood of the martyrs of Jesus."*

18:20-24 As Babylon the Great is being destroyed, the saints, apostles and **prophets** are called upon to rejoice *"for God hath avenged you on her."* God destroyed her because *"in her was found the blood of **prophets**, and of saints, and of all that were slain upon the earth."*

Based upon these verses, we conclude that the destruction of **Babylon the Great** comes as vengeance from God because the blood of saints and **prophets** and of all that were slain upon the earth were found in her. When it was accomplished, it was to be understood as God's avenging of His holy apostles and prophets.

The Vengeance Promised by Jesus

Let us remember that the book of Revelation contains the message given to John by Jesus Christ through His angel. Jesus gave the same message to His apostles during His personal ministry.

Luke 13:31-33 This text is probably hyperbole, but it means something. Jesus said, *"It cannot be that a **prophet** perish out of Jerusalem."* What did he mean? He certainly did not mean that all prophets died in Jerusalem because they did not all die there. What He meant must be understood from the standpoint that Jerusalem was the capital of Israel and was held responsible for the misdeeds of the nation. Jesus was simply saying He would die in Jerusalem to seal the doom of the nation. As far as we know, the nation of Israel was responsible for the death of **all the prophets.**

Luke 11:45-51 In this text, Jesus stated that He would send prophets and apostles to the nation of Israel and some of them they would persecute and slay, *"That the blood of **all the prophets,** which was shed from the foundation of the world, may be required of this generation."*

Matthew 23:29-39 In this scathing denunciation of the Jewish leaders, Jesus accused the Jews of being responsible for the death of the prophets. He said, *"O Jerusalem, Jerusalem, **thou that killest the prophets,** and stonest them which are sent unto thee."*

In concluding our findings, we have observed that Jerusalem would be destroyed as vengeance from God. She would be destroyed because in her was found the blood of **all the prophets,** in fact, **all the righteous blood shed upon the earth.** This would be required of the generation living when Jesus spoke these words.

When the two messages are considered together, they are identical. There is no difference. Therefore, we must conclude that **Babylon the Great** of the book of Revelation is **symbolic** of **Jerusalem** and can be none other. All of the characteristics of Babylon only fit Jerusalem. Since the city, destroyed in the second division of the book, is the city **where our Lord was crucified** and compares with Babylon the Great of the third division, then, Jerusalem must be the city under consideration.

This argument cannot be successfully denied. It has stood the test thus far and establishes the primary subject matter of the Apocalypse. The book of Revelation centers around the desolation of the nation of Israel and the destruction of Jerusalem.

Home Exercise

This exercise deals with the titles, names and designations by which Jesus Christ is identified in the book of Revelation.

Fill in the Blanks and Supply the Verse(s) Where Found

1. *"These things saith the _____, the faithful and true _____, the _____ of the _____ of God."*
Ch/Vs _____

2. *"These things saith he that is _____, he that is _____, he that hath the _____ of David."*
Ch/Vs _____

3. *"I am the root and the _____ of _____, and the bright and morning _____."*
Ch/Vs _____

4. *"I am _____ and _____, the beginning and the _____, the _____ and the _____."* Ch/Vs _____, _____, _____.

5. *"The Lord God Almighty and the _____ are the temple of it..., and the Lamb is the _____ thereof."* Ch/Vs _____

6. New Jerusalem was *"prepared as a bride adorned for her _____."*
Ch/Vs _____

7. *"One like unto the Son of _____."*   Ch/Vs _____
"These things saith the Son of _____."   Ch/Vs _____

8. *"The kingdoms of this world are become the kingdoms of our _____, and of his _____."*   Ch/Vs _____

9. *"He that sat upon him was called _____ and _____."*
Ch/Vs _____

10. *"He hath on his vesture and on his thigh a name written, _____ of _____ and _____ of _____."* Ch/Vs _____

11. *"Weep not: behold, the _____ of the _____ of Juda, the _____ of _____, hath prevailed."*   Ch/Vs _____

Lesson 4

Background to the Apocalyptic Message

We have established that the purpose of the Apocalypse is to show the desolation of the nation of Israel and the destruction of Jerusalem. Now, it will be helpful to understand the background that made the book of Revelation a necessary part of the New Testament. This background is identified when the mighty angel declared, *"But in the days of the voice of the seventh angel, when he shall begin to sound, the mystery of God should be finished, as he hath declared to his servants the prophets"* (Rev.10:7).

The word **mystery (musterion)** means "a hidden or secret thing, not obvious to the understanding; a hidden purpose or counsel; secret will."[8] God's will was **a hidden or secret thing** not obvious to the understanding in the Old Testament. Paul called it **"hidden wisdom...which none of the princes of this world knew"** (1 Cor.2:7-8). It was **"kept secret"** (Rom.16:25), **"hid in God"** (Eph.3:9), **"from ages and from generations"** (Col.1:26), and **"not made known unto the sons of men"** (Eph.3:5). It is not a mystery today, however, because **"God hath revealed them unto us by his Spirit"** (1 Cor.2:10; cf.Rom.16:26; Col.1:26; Eph.3:3-5,9). So, the mystery of God declared to his servants the prophets was made known (Rev.10:7). It is revealed in the New Testament.

The Nation of Israel in God's Plan

God works all things after the counsel of his will (Eph.1:11; cf.Acts 2:23; 4:28; Rev.4:11). What He does is governed by carefully orchestrated plans. When Adam transgressed God's law in the Garden, God immediately revealed plans to bruise Satan through the seed of woman and lift man from his fallen state (Gen.3:15). The plan was hidden, and man did not understand it, but God has revealed it unto us today (cf.Rev.12:1-9). Throughout the Old Testament we see God unfolding His plan and accomplishing His purpose to raise man from his fallen state through our Lord Jesus Christ (Rom.7:24-25; 8:1-2).

---

[8] Thayer, *MUSTERION*, page 420.

About 2,000 years B.C., God selected Abraham and made him two significant promises. First, God promised to make of Abraham a great nation and, second, He promised that through Abraham's seed all nations of the earth would be blessed (Gen.12:1-3). The first promise was fulfilled through Abraham's grandson, Jacob, whose name God changed to Israel. Jacob begat twelve sons who became the foundation of the nation of Israel. In Egypt, Abraham's descendants grew into a large nation. Under the leadership of Moses they were delivered from Egyptian oppression and, at Sinai, given a national, civil and religious law to govern them. Through this nation God developed the **seed of Abraham** through which He blessed all nations (Gal.3:8-21).

God's Covenant With Israel

God made it abundantly clear that Israel as a nation would be blessed as long as they obeyed His covenant but, if they disobeyed and followed other gods, curses would follow. While many texts from Exodus 19 through Deuteronomy deal with this covenant, Deuteronomy 28:1-32:44 clearly spells out what the outcome would be if Israel chose to disobey. The history of Israel over the 1500 years of their existence is outlined for us. It is one of the most amazing texts in the Old Testament. The class would do well to study this text carefully, placing emphasis upon God's promises to consume and destroy the people off the land. He promised also to carry them into captivities; return them to the land upon their repentance, and bring them to their latter end as He avenged His servants upon His enemies. Special emphasis should also be given to the song Moses taught Israel (Deut.32:1-44). The passage is important because it shows the 1500 year history of Israel until their end in 70 A.D.

Jerusalem

Jerusalem entered the picture several hundred years later when Israel's second king, David, made Jerusalem the capital of the kingdom (2 Sam.5:5-10). Afterward, God chose Jerusalem as the place for His name to dwell (2 Chron.6:1-6). Solomon built God's temple according to His plan. This elevated Jerusalem to a position of prominence in Israel. It was called the **city of God** and **the holy city.** Because it was the capital of the nation and the center of God's worship, He soon held Jerusalem responsible for the sins of the nation.

The sins of Israel led the ten northern tribes into the Assyrian captivity in 721 B.C. and the sins of Judah led them into captivity in Babylon in 605 B.C. The maximum punishment for Israel was the destruction of Jerusalem by the Babylonians in 586 B.C. God's servants the prophets warned Israel to repent or be punished. They refused and God's punishment came and was severe.

Restoration

In 539 B.C., the Medes and Persians conquered the Babylonians and permitted the Jews who wished to return to Judea to rebuild the temple at Jerusalem. Later, the city and its walls were rebuilt (Ezra, Nehemiah). After many years, the restoration was complete. Jerusalem was rebuilt and ultimately regained it's power and influence in the world as it served as the religious capital of Judaism until it's destruction in 70 A.D.

Prophecies of Jerusalem's Final Destruction

The Old Testament scriptures are filled with warnings from God of the dangerous course His people followed. He sent the prophets Joel, Amos, Hosea, Micah, Isaiah, Zephaniah, Habakkuk and Jeremiah to warn the people and call them back to God. Israel, Judah and Jerusalem were pictured as committing gross whoredom. Ezekiel portrayed them all in whoredom by an allegory of two women answering in comparison to **Samaria** and **Jerusalem** (Ezek.23). Time and again they were accused of whoredom until they were consumed and carried captive to foreign lands with their cities and land ravished, destroyed and lying desolate. The curses Moses promised came to pass.

The captivities of Israel and Judah and the destruction of Jerusalem did not fulfill all that God promised. He had promised them an end, a **latter end,** which was yet to come (Deut.32:20,29). God's servants the prophets reflect it. Study the following texts carefully. They must be applied to the destruction of Jerusalem in 70 A.D.

Isaiah 65 This text, dated around 700 B.C. shows God's intention to punish Israel following the salvation of the Gentiles. A new heaven and earth were promised with a new Jerusalem. This is the message of Revelation.

Daniel 9:24-27 Jerusalem lay in a heap of ruins from her destruction in 586 B.C. when Daniel received this information. He was told Jerusalem would be rebuilt and destroyed again.

Other Old Testament texts also pointing to the destruction of Jerusalem in 70 A.D. are: Isa.24-27; 28:18-22; 29; 48:9; 62:2; 66:1-6,15-18; Jer.30:5-10; Dan.7:21-27; Hos.6:11; Joel 2:28-32; Zech.14:1-7.

The Teaching of Jesus and the Apostles

Several Old Testament texts could be cited but these demonstrate our point. As you continue your study, carefully consider all of the following texts in the New Testament. These prove that the destruction of Jerusalem was planned by God and would come during the lifetime of those living when Jesus was upon earth: Matt.22:1-10; 23:29-39; 24; Mk.13; Lk.11:45-52; 13:1-9,28-35; 19:41-44; 21:5-36; 23:28-31; Acts 3:19-21; 6:13-14; 13:40-41; Rom.9:19-24,27-28; 1 Thess.2:14-16; Heb.12:25-27.

Conclusion

God's plan was designed to bring the **Savior** into the world. The nation of Israel was God's special people through whom this Messiah would come. Once that nation had served its purpose, it was no longer needed and, because they left God, He brought them to their ultimate end. This act on God's part served to seal up prophecy and prove that the Messiah had come (Dan.9:24-27); precisely the message of Revelation 10:7.

Home Exercise

1. List three principle characters in ch. 1: _____,
_____, _____.

2. Name four persons mentioned in ch. 2: _____,
_____, _____, _____.

3. Which verse in ch. 3 ties in with ch. 20? _____

4. Which verse in ch. 4 ties in with ch. 15? _____

5. Who is the principle character of ch. 5? _____

6. List the different colored things of ch. 6: _____
_____
_____

7. Which tribe of Israel is missing in ch. 7? _____

8. List the things in ch. 8 that fly: _____

9. Give the Greek name for the angel of the bottomless pit (ch.9):
_____ Its Meaning: _____

10. Who was told to eat a book in ch. 10? _____

11. Name the city destroyed in ch. 11: _____

12. Name four principle characters in ch. 12: _____,
_____, _____, _____.

13. Name the two entities introduced in ch. 13: _____
_____, _____.

14. How many angelic messages in ch. 14? _____

15. If you were giving a brief title to chs 15 & 16, what would it be?
_____

16. What reason is given in chs 17 & 18 for the destruction of
Babylon? _____
_____

17. Name the things destroyed in chs 19 & 20: _____
_____
_____

18. List three outstanding characteristics of new Jerusalem (chs
21-22): _____
_____
_____

These exercises are designed to acquaint you with the text of the
book of Revelation. If you work your exercises, you will be ready to
study the text.

PART II

The Textual Study

You are now ready to begin your study of the text of the book of Revelation. Please remember the four divisions of the book as you study: (1) The Seven Churches of Asia, (2) The Heavenly Apocalypse, (3) The Earthly Apocalypse, and (4) The New Jerusalem. The first and last sections are related and you should watch for the things which show that relationship. The second and third sections are also related and you should observe the points of likeness in these sections also.

Remember, the Lord promises to bless you in your study of this book (1:3). Put forth the maximum effort and receive the maximum blessing.

Lesson 5

Chapter 1

The Revelation of Jesus Christ

Prologue

Vv. 1-3 This section of the book appears to have been added after the Apocalypse was written. John had already testified of all the things he had seen (1:2). Verse 4 is the natural beginning of the book.

The prologue affirms three things of note. First, the Apocalypse came from God through our Lord Jesus Christ as given to John by His angel. Second, blessedness awaits those who read and/or hear its message and keep the things revealed therein. Third, the time for its fulfillment was at hand when John received it.

Salutatory Address

Vv. 4-5a The Apocalypse was addressed to the seven churches of Asia (cf.1:11 for names). There were other churches in Asia (Col.4:13). Perhaps the Lord named only seven in order to use the numerical symbol **seven.** It symbolizes the **complete** or **whole.** The seven churches, therefore, represent all of the churches.

John brings greetings from the Father, the **seven spirits** of God, (i.e., the Holy Spirit, cf.4:5; 5:6), and Jesus Christ, who is **the faithful witness, the first begotten of the dead,** and **the prince of the kings of the earth.**

Praises of Glory and Dominion unto Christ

Vv. 5b-6 Christ is judged worthy of **glory and dominion** because (1) He loved us (cf.Jn.15:12; 2 Cor.5:14; Eph.3:19; 5:2), (2) washed us from our sins in His blood (Matt.26:28; Lk.24:46-47; Acts 2:38; 22:16; Rom.6:3-4), and (3) made us kings and priests unto God (1 Pet.2:5,9). He is worthy of our praise for ever and ever.

Christ in Judgment

V. 7 Throughout the book of Revelation, Jesus is portrayed coming in judgment (cf.2:5,25; 3:3,10-11; 16:15; 22:7,12,20). His coming would be quick and unexpected. Its purpose was to try them that dwelt upon the earth (3:10).

This coming of the Lord was not the expected second coming of Christ (cf.1 Thess.3:13; 4:13-17; 2 Thess.1:7-10). Careful study will reveal a likeness in this text to passages promising Jesus' coming in the destruction of Jerusalem (Matt.24:30; 26:64). This judgment is the kind often spoken of in the Old Testament where God was pictured coming upon clouds (cf.Isa.19:1; Jer.4:14-14; Ezek.30:3-4,18; 34:12-13; Joel 2:2; Zeph.1:15). Special attention should be given to those who **pierced Him** and the **kindreds** (tribes) of the earth (land) who mourn because of him.

Divine Sanction

V. 8 John evidently gave his sanction to the promised judgment when he said, *"Even so, Amen."* God gave His sanction also by identifying Himself as the Almighty, Eternal one. Alpha and Omega are the first and last letters in the Greek alphabet. God is saying, "I am the beginning, the end, and everything in between." When we apply this to the Apocalypse, we see God, who formed the nation of Israel to serve His purposes, bringing that nation to its end at His appointed time (cf.Rev.4:11).

John's Circumstances and Commission

Vv. 9-11 John tells about himself and his circumstances. He is a **brother** and **companion in tribulation**, a partner together with them as citizens **in the kingdom and patience of (in) Jesus Christ.** Tribulation was to precede the destruction of Jerusalem (Matt.24:21,29; Mk.13:24; cf.Rev.7:14), which in turn was a sign the Messiah and His kingdom had come (Dan.9:24-27). John being in the kingdom and patience in Christ affirms that the Messiah and His kingdom made their appearance (Lk.21:19,29-32).

John was confined to a rocky, desolate island five miles wide by ten miles long located 24 miles off the coast of Asia known as Patmos. It was about 70 miles southwest of Ephesus. John was evidently there as a prisoner.

John was transposed to be **in the Spirit.** This is the posture in which John received the visions (4:2; 17:3; 21:10; cf.2 Cor.12:2-3). John saw the vision on (in) **the Lord's day** which many think was Sunday. Another explanation is possible. The Apocalypse reveals God's wrath being poured upon the persecutors of His people. In the Old Testament, such outpouring of wrath is called **the day of the Lord** (Joel 1:15; 2:1-11; 3:14). In Revelation we read that *"the great day of his* (the Lamb's) *wrath is come"* (6:17). This indicates that the day of wrath is the Lord's day. This is contextually correct and reasonable.

John heard a voice like a trumpet. The trumpet signifies a warning (cf.Ezek.33:3-6; Joel 2:1; Jer.4:19-20). Wrath was coming. John was instructed to write a book and send it to the seven churches of Asia.

The Vision of Christ Among the Lampstands

Vv. 12-20 John saw a vision personage who identified Himself with God as *"the Alpha and Omega, the first and the last."* He was standing in the midst of seven golden lampstands. John described Him in glorious terms as like the **son of man** (cf.Dan.7,10). He was clothed down to the feet. He wore a golden girdle. His head and hairs were white; His eyes as a flame of fire; His feet like fine brass; His voice as many waters; His right hand held seven stars; a sharp two-edged sword protruded out of His mouth and His countenance was as bright as the sun.

The scene pictures the Son of God in His present position as King of Kings, Lord of Lords, and High Priest. He is in the midst of the churches holding their angels (messengers) in His right hand (v.20). What a beautiful picture of God and his Son in our midst.

Home Exercise
Chapter 1

MULTIPLE CHOICE:

1. Alpha and Omega are (cities of Asia; letters of the Greek Alphabet; ferocious animals).
2. Jesus now has the keys of (hell and death; the kingdom; heaven).
3. When John saw the son of man he (died; fainted; fell at his feet).
4. The Holy Spirit is identified as (seven spirits; the Almighty; the Alpha and Omega).
5. The things John revealed were (2000 years away; never to happen; at hand).
6. Patmos was (a city; an island; an ancient country).

MATCHING:

1. _____ Angels	a.	paps
2. _____ Jesus Christ	b.	White like wool
3. _____ Patmos	c.	Eyes
4. _____ Voice	d.	Right hand
5. _____ Countenance	e.	golden
6. _____ Head & hairs	f.	sun
7. _____ Feet	g.	like a trumpet
8. _____ Flame of fire	h.	fine brass
9. _____ Golden Girdle	i.	John
10. _____ Candlesticks	j.	Faithful witness

FILL IN THE BLANKS:

1. John said he was a "_____, and _____ in tribulation, and in the _____ and patience of _____."

2. John saw the first vision while "in the _____ on the _____."

3. John said he saw "_____ golden _____ " and "one like unto the _____ of _____ " in their midst.

4. In the coming of Jesus described in chapter one, it is said that "_____ _____ shall see him, and they also which _____."

5. John bore "record of the _____ of God, and of the _____ of Jesus Christ, and of _____ _____ that he saw."

Lesson 6

Chapter 2

Epistles to the Churches

Introduction

Portrayed in His divine position as our **King** and **High Priest,** Jesus Christ addressed the seven churches of Asia. Except for the last two churches, He identified Himself with the vision personage of chapter 1. To Philadelphia, He affiliated Himself with Old Testament prophecy (Isa.22:21-22) and, to Laodicea, He equated Himself with New Testament teaching (Jn.1:3; 2 Cor.1:20; Rev.1:5). When all of the distinguishing statements are considered, it is evident that Jesus Christ, the Son of God, was addressing the churches.

Jesus knows our works. Every church and its works are known unto Him. Nothing escapes His eyes (Heb.4:13). Such knowledge of our lives and our services should motivate us to genuine obedience.

Jesus **commended** the churches when commendation was warranted. He found something good in all except Laodicea. He also **condemned** them when condemnation was called for. He found something in all to condemn except Smyrna and Philadelphia. How does He view your congregation? Remember, a church is what its members make it. Are you what you ought to be?

Jesus called upon all of the churches who were not walking uprightly to **repent.** Warnings were sounded lest His call fall on deaf ears. Blessings were promised those who **overcome.** Incentives are abundant for those who wish to do right.

All of the churches were exhorted to **hear what the Spirit saith unto the churches.** While Jesus recognized the areas wherein the churches were astray, He directed them to listen to the Spirit for instructions on how to do His will. What the Spirit said to the churches is found in our New Testament Scriptures. Search for these things as you study the churches.

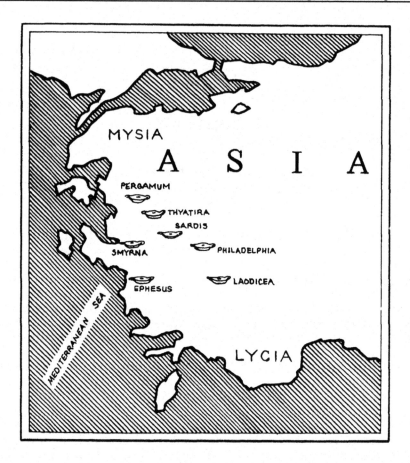

Ephesus

Vv. 1-7 Ephesus was located about 70 miles northeast of Patmos. It was the capital of the Roman province of Asia, and a prosperous business center. Its magnificent temple of Diana was one of the seven wonders of the ancient world. The church was started in Ephesus when Paul journeyed there with Aquila and Priscilla at the close of his second missionary journey (Acts 18:18). On his third missionary journey, Paul spent three years in Ephesus (cf.Acts 19; 20:31).

The church at Ephesus was a good church by most standards. They had **worked hard, patiently endured trials, hated evil, and tried and convicted false apostles.** Not many churches we know can measure up to that kind of commendation, yet the Lord said to them, *"Nevertheless I have somewhat against thee."*

The reason: *"Thou hast left thy first love."* This was a good church but they had become slack in their effort. It was not what it used to be. The Lord called upon them to **repent** or He would **remove their lampstand.**

Smyrna

Vv. 8-11 Smyrna was located about 35 miles north and west of Ephesus. It rivaled Ephesus in size and beauty. A temple dedicated to the worship of Rome had been located in Smyrna since 195 B.C. and a temple for the worship of Emperor Augustus was erected there in 25 B.C. Its relationship to the sea and the interior of Asia made it a very prosperous city. Nothing is known of the church in Smyrna apart from this epistle.

This church was known for **its works, tribulation, and poverty.** Their suffering had evidently come from the Jews who **blasphemed** them. Their poverty could have also been caused by their persecutors.

"But thou art rich." They were not rich materially but spiritually (cf.Eph.1:3,7,18; 1 Tim.6:17-18; Jas.2:5). These people were rich with the kind of riches that really count. Because of this the Lord promised that their future trials would be light (ten days) and if they remained faithful to death they would receive **a crown of life.**

Pergamos

Vv. 12-17 Pergamos was located 55 miles north of Smyrna. It was situated on a huge rocky hill in the Caicus River valley 15 miles from the sea-coast. It was filled with temples and altars to the gods. A temple dedicated to the worship of Emperor Augustus in 29 B.C. was also there. Nothing is known of the church in Pergamos apart from this epistle.

This church experienced hard times. **Satan's seat** was there. This probably refers to the temples already mentioned or to the temple dedicated to the worship of **Asklepios**, the god of healing who was worshiped as a living serpent. **Antipas** had been martyred but it had not shaken their faith. They **held fast to the Lord's name and did not deny his faith.** This was a good church except for the fact that they permitted some of their number to hold to the doctrines of Balaam and the Nicolaitans. Holding to false doctrine is a serious offense (2 Jn.9-11). The Lord called upon them to **repent** or suffer the consequences.

Thyatira

Vv. 18-29 Thyatira was located about 35 miles southeast of Pergamos. It was the smallest of the seven cities and of less political importance. It was a thriving commercial center noted for weavers, tanners, dyers, potters, clothiers, cobblers, bakers, bronze-workers and many more. Trade-guilds were formed, having their own guardian gods. These gods were worshiped by sacrifices, huge festivals and immoral practices. Nothing is known about the church apart from this epistle. Lydia (Acts 16:14-15) was from this city.

This church was known for its **charity, service, faith, patience and works.** It was a good church except for their tolerance of a woman named **Jezebel** who taught and seduced the Lord's servants to engage in idolatrous and immoral practices. She and her converts were called upon to **repent** of their sinful practices or suffer the consequences, and the church was held responsible for permitting her to continue unchecked. The Lord expects His people to discipline false teachers.

Home Exercise
Chapter 2

TRUE OR FALSE:
1. _____ Jesus is identified as the Son of God.
2. _____ The church at Smyrna was materially wealthy.
3. _____ Jezebel was a prophetess.
4. _____ Balaam taught Balac to lead Israel into sin.
5. _____ The Jews are called the synagogue of Satan.
6. _____ The Ephesian church hated false teachers.
7. _____ The tree of life is said to be in heaven.
8. _____ Antipas was a faithful martyr which means he died because he was a Christian.
9. _____ While the Lord hated the doctrine of the Nicolaitanes He tolerated it.
10. _____ Jezebel was not given opportunity to repent.

QUESTIONS:
1. What expression to each church indicates the omniscience of Jesus? _____
2. Which church (chapter 2) was acceptable to Jesus? _____
3. What expression used four times emphasizes the role of the Holy Spirit in the New Testament? _____
4. What did the Lord want the churches to learn from Jezebel's punishment? _____
5. What is the second death (cf.Rev.20:6,14)? _____
6. What were three churches in chapter two called upon to do that Smyrna did not need to do? _____
7. What does the overcomer receive that no one else knows he has? _____

MATCH TO THE CHURCHES:
1. _____ crown   7. _____ Antipas
2. _____ Satan dwells   8. _____ charity
3. _____ hated evil   9. _____ tribulation
4. _____ Jezebel   10. _____ left 1st love
5. _____ rich   11. _____ holds my name
6. _____ service   12. _____ false apostle

a. Ephesus b. Smyrna c. Pergamos d. Thyatira

Lesson 7

Chapter 3

The Epistles Continued

Sardis

Vv. 1-6 Sardis was located 30 miles south-southeast of Thyatira at the foot of Mt. Tmolus in the fertile valley of the Hermus river. It was a busy center for trade and traffic. Nothing is known of the church in Sardis apart from this epistle.

Only Laodicea carried a name more disgraceful than Sardis. She had **a name that she lived, but was dead.** This church was very active in works, but the works were not the ones the Lord had ordained (Eph.2:10; 2 Tim.3:16-17). The Lord said, **"I have not found thy works perfect before God."** The word **perfect** means **complete.** So, this church was busy, but it was not busy completing the Lord's works. The Christians at Sardis were to **strengthen the things remaining, remember how they had received and heard, hold fast, and repent** or suffer the consequences.

Philadelphia

Vv. 7-13 Continuing east-southeast from Sardis 25 miles would bring one to Philadelphia. This was the city built by the Greeks as a center to spread the Greek language and culture in Lydia and Phrygia. It was in a rich farming region. We know nothing of this church apart from this epistle.

The Lord opened a door to Philadelphia that could not be closed. He praised them for their **strength,** though it was **little,** and their fidelity to His **word** and **name.** They had remained loyal in the face of severe trials from the Jews. For this He promised deliverance from the **hour of temptation** which would come upon the earth. This period of reference could be identified with the period of tribulation which was to precede the destruction of Jerusalem (cf.Matt.24:21-29). Supporting this conclusion is the Lord's promise to **"come quickly"** frequently made in the Apocalypse.

Laodicea

Vv. 14-22 Located 40 miles southeast of Philadelphia, and about 100 miles east of Ephesus, was Laodicea, a city of wealth and many luxuries. It was noted for its hot springs and medical school which in turn was famous for its eye salve and ear ointment. Laodicea was stationed at the junction of three great highways which contributed to its commercial and financial growth. We know nothing of the church in Laodicea apart from this epistle.

Our Lord had nothing good to say about this church. They were **lukewarm** which means they were filled with apathy and indifference. They reasoned that, because they were **rich, increased with goods, and had need of nothing** materially, they were all right with God. What a mistake! Their lack of real concern blinded them to their true condition of being **wretched, and miserable, and poor, and blind, and naked.** They were charged to produce fruit: **gold tried in the fire, white raiment, anointed eyes** and **repentance.** Though this church did not measure up to the Lord's expectations, He held out hope for repentance which would open the door for continued fellowship.

Summary

We now have an understanding of how the churches are seen by the Son of God. Looking down from heaven He sees, hears and knows. The way in which He described each church with their individual personalities convinces us of His full knowledge of all things, even the smallest individual activity.

We also know what it takes to please Him by observing the points of commendation in the churches. They were commended for their love, service, faith, works, life, purity, strength and patience, all of which are necessary to acceptability to Him.

We also learned what displeases the Lord. He does not tolerate **second place**, and He does not approve of indifference, worldliness, immorality, ignorance, incomplete works, error, or the tolerance of error. Any one of these points of condemnation is sufficient grounds for a threat of judgment and a call for repentance.

Abundant blessings are promised those who **overcome**: the right to **the tree of life** (2:7); **no second death** (2:11); **a white stone** (2:17); **power over the nations** (2:26); **the morning star** (2:28); **white raiment, name in the book of life and acknowledgment before the Father and angels** (3:5); **a new name, the name of God and new Jerusalem in which he becomes a pillar and shall go no more out** (3:12), and

reigning with Christ on His throne (3:21). What an incentive to do right!

Who is the **overcomer** and when does he obtain the right to enjoy these blessings? The Greek word for **overcome** means *"to conquer...; a. absol. to carry off the victory, come off victorious."*[9] Overcomers gain the victory, but what victory and when? We are prone to think only in terms of the **ultimate** victory which comes after death, but John's use, unless contextually specified (cf.2:26), always refers to the **present** victory. These blessings for the most part are enjoyed **now** by the **overcomer.** We reign with Christ **now.** When earth life ends, the reign of Christ will be over (1 Cor.15:24-28), therefore, this blessing must be realized in this present age.

Finally, by presenting the seven churches for observation, the Lord has given us a picture of the church on earth in its local, physical (fleshly) and imperfect essence. In the final chapters (21-22), we will consider the church in its universal, spiritual and perfect essence. It may be said that the church is pictured in chapters 2-3 with members who have not fully **overcome,** while chapters 21-22 view the church only from the standpoint of the **overcomers.** (In order to see the relationship between the first and last sections of Revelation, it would be advantageous to read chapters 21-22 at this point.)

---

[9] Thayer, *NIKAO*, page 425.

Home Exercise
Chapter 3

TRUE OR FALSE:

1. _____ Jesus identifies Himself as the creator.
2. _____ New Jerusalem is pictured as being in heaven.
3. _____ Christians at Laodicea were materially rich.
4. _____ Some Christians in Sardis wore white robes.
5. _____ An hour of trial was promised upon the world.
6. _____ Jesus is pictured as an overcomer.
7. _____ Christians at Laodicea walked around naked.
8. _____ Jews would worship at the feet of Christians.
9. _____ Jesus promised to make some overcomers cornerstones in the temple of God.
10. _____ Those who wear white robes also have their names written in the book of life.

QUESTIONS:

1. Which church in chapter 3 was acceptable to Jesus? _____

2. What problem was found with the church at Sardis? _____

3. What problem was found with Philadelphia? _____

4. What problem was found with Laodicea? _____

5. List the blessings promised overcomers in ch. 3: _____

6. For what purpose was an hour of temptation coming? _____

7. What does it take to make us really rich? _____

8. Which church did Jesus threaten to sneak up on? _____

MATCH TO THE CHURCHES:

1. ___ book of life   5. ___ an open door   9. ___ lukewarm
2. ___ ready to die   6. ___ strength   10. ___ dead
3. ___ kept my word   7. ___ be zealous   11. ___ crown
4. ___ need nothing   8. ___ anoint eyes   12. ___ repent

a. Sardis   b. Philadelphia   c. Laodicea

Lesson 8
Chapter 4

The Old Testament Throne Scene
Introduction

The stage has been set to unveil **the things shortly to come to pass.** The Godhead was introduced as the source of the message to be revealed (1:4-8), and Jesus Christ specifically introduced in His role as King ruling and reigning with all authority among the churches (1:11-20). The churches were viewed in their particular circumstances as either prepared or unprepared for the events soon to *"come upon all the world to try them that dwell upon the earth"* (3:10). We are now ready for the angel to reveal the historical events being foretold.

We call this section of Revelation (chapters 4-11) **The Heavenly Apocalypse.** John first portrays the throne of God as the Lamb assumes control. Then he depicts the desolation of the nation of Israel and the destruction of Jerusalem as ordered and directed by that throne (cf.6:16-17). When the smoke of God's wrath clears, God and Christ are praised for having demonstrated their righteous rule (11:15-18).

John's Visionary Posture

Vv. 1-2a John observed as Christ addressed the churches standing among the lampstands. The vision was complete and is not linked to the other visions. Another scene in this great production now unfolds. A door opened in heaven, and John was invited to enter and see **the things which would be hereafter.** Flesh and blood cannot enter the heavenly realm (1 Cor.15:50), so, immediately John was in the spirit, the proper posture for seeing visions (cf.2 Cor.12:1-4). John was **in the spirit** when he saw the first vision (1:10; Lesson 5, p.23).

The Throne

Vv. 2b-8a When John entered the door he was in the throne room of heaven. On His throne, God appeared as a **jasper** and **sardius**

stone; beautiful to behold. A **rainbow** encircled the throne as ravishing as an **emerald.** Twenty-four **elders** sat upon 24 **thrones** around the throne clothed in **white** and on their heads **crowns of gold.** Proceeding out of the throne were **lightnings, thunderings and voices. Seven burning lamps,** and a **sea of glass as clear as crystal,** were before the throne, and there were **four beasts** (actually living things) in the midst and surrounding the throne. It was a majestic scene which only a few have been privileged to see (cf.Isa.6:1-4; Ezek.1:26-28; Dan.7:9-14).

What does all of this mean? Remember, John was seeing a vision! He did not see literal heaven, but what he saw was designed to give us a glorious message about heaven. God is presented in all of His majestic splendor and glory. The rainbow apparently symbolizes God's **faithfulness** (cf.Gen.9:8-17). The **living things** were a part of God's throne and represent the **attributes** of God and the all-sidedness of His nature. The lightnings, thunderings and voices signify **great power and energies** emanating from the throne of God.

The other details of John's vision are designed to associate our understanding with God's rule under the Mosaic era (cf.Heb.9:1-10,23-24; 10:1). The lamps burning before the throne correspond to the golden candlesticks in the Holy Place of the Temple. The lamps were the **seven spirits of God,** or the Holy Spirit. The twenty-four Elders around the throne very reasonably compare to the twenty-four orders of priests appointed by King David to carry out the worship of Israel as directed to God (1 Chron.24-25). If so, the twenty-four Elders represent the acceptable worship of Israel as personified in the presence of God. The sea of glass before the throne relates to the **brazen sea** of Solomon's Temple (cf.1 Chron.4:2-22) in which the priests cleansed themselves prior to entering the temple (2 Chron.4:6). It symbolizes the necessary cleansing of all who approach God's throne.

Four **living things** with **six wings** full of eyes before and behind were in the middle and around the throne. One was like a lion, another like a calf, one had the face of a man and one was like a flying eagle. Again, this is a vision and reveals the nature and character of God and His throne. God is omniscient, omnipotent, omnipresent, eternal, holy, just, righteous, loving, merciful, gentle, kind, faithful, resolute, fierce and consuming. He must be feared and reverenced.

Heavenly Praise

Vv. 8b-11 The living things praised God continually in the midst of the throne. Since the living things symbolize God's great attributes, the scene teaches us that God is praised by His own power, glory and majesty. These praise Him because every manifestation of God's greatness draws praise from all of His creation when observed.

The living things praise God continually. John sees them in a special demonstration of God's power – a special outburst of praise. When this happens, the 24 Elders fall prostrate before God casting their crowns before the throne. When special demonstrations of God's power were manifest, such as in the Assyrian and Babylonian captivities, Israel always came crawling back heaping their sincere praises upon God. Why? Because God created all things for His **will.** God's actions are evidence of purpose and will. The historical events about to be unveiled were a part of God's will. God is praised because these things, when carried out, are recognized as ordered and directed by the throne of God in heaven.

Summary

John has given us a view of the throne of God as it once existed. In chapter 5, we will see the throne as it is changed by the appearance of Jesus Christ as the Lamb of God. Because of this transformation, we must view chapter 4 as a picture of the throne of God as it existed under the Old Testament era.

Home Exercise
Chapter 4

FILL IN THE BLANKS:

1. *"Out of the throne proceeded _____ and _____ and _____."*

2. *" _____, _____, _____, ____ ____ _____, which was, and is, and is to come."*

3. *"Thou art _____, O _____, to receive _____ and _____ and _____."*

4. *"A _____ was _____ in _____: and the first _____ which I heard was ____ it were of a _____ talking with me."*

DESCRIBE THE FOLLOWING:

1. The one on the throne: _____

2. The Throne (in the midst and around it): _____

3. The 24 Elders: _____

4. The first beast (or living being): _____

5. The second beast (or living being): _____

6. The third beast (or living being): _____

7. The fourth beast (or living being): _____

MATCHING:

1. _____ Crowns of Gold	a.	Thunderings-voices
2. _____ Full of eyes	b.	In heaven
3. _____ Sea of Glass	c.	The Beasts
4. _____ Seven Spirits	d.	Wings
5. _____ Twenty-four	e.	Holy, Holy, Holy
6. _____ Trumpet	f.	Rainbow
7. _____ Emerald	g.	Twenty-four Elders
8. _____ Never rest	h.	Fourth Beast
9. _____ Lord God Almighty	i.	Seven lamps of fire
10. _____ A throne	j.	Seats or thrones
11. _____ Lightnings	k.	Voice
12. _____ Flying Eagle	l.	Crystal

Lesson 9

Chapter 5

The New Testament Throne Scene

The Search for One
Worthy to Open the Book

Having established the rule of God as it existed under the Mosaic age chapter five begins with the introduction of the New Testament period. Christ appeared as the Lamb, received the revelation of God's fully sealed word, and commenced His rule and reign as King of kings and Lord of lords. All of heaven and earth submit to Him.

Vv. 1-5 John observed that God had a book (scroll) in His right hand written on both sides. It was full, and sealed with seven seals. A search was made for one worthy to loose the seals and open the scroll but no one in all of heaven or earth was found. This upset John who wept until one of the  elders comforted him with the news that the Lion of the tribe of Judah, the Root of David, had **overcome** and was worthy to open the book and loose its seals.

The scroll in God's right hand represents the full and complete purposes of God which He ordained before the foundation of the world (1 Cor.2:7-9). They were revealed to us by Jesus Christ through the Spirit (Rom.16:25-26). Jesus revealed some of the mystery while He was with His apostles (Jn.17:6-8) but not all. He promised to complete the task by sending the Holy Spirit when He ascended to the Father (Jn.16:12-15). Our scene pictures Christ accomplishing this.

The scroll was sealed with **seven seals.** A seal on a document establishes it as genuine. Seven seals indicates complete genuineness. The seals are signs, or proofs, of the book's source. As we shall see, the seals symbolize historical events which prove that God's eternal purposes, as preserved and revealed for us in the Bible, are indeed from God in heaven.

Jesus as the Lion of the tribe of Judah came in fulfillment of Jacob's blessing to Judah (Gen.49:8-10). His identification with the Root of David shows Him as the Messiah of Old Testament prophecy (2 Sam.7:12-16; Lk.1:68-70). Jesus is pictured in our study coming to God's throne in the fulfillment of all Old Testament messianic prophecy.

The Lamb at the Right Hand of God

Vv. 6-7 John looked and saw Jesus Christ appear in the midst of the throne as a Lamb that had been slain having **seven horns and seven eyes.** He came to God's right hand where He took the scroll from the Father.

John was viewing the advent of Christ to the throne of God following His death and resurrection. After offering himself as a sacrifice for our sins, Jesus took His position at God's right hand (Heb.1:3; 9:12,24; 10:12). He was given all authority in heaven and earth as symbolized by the **seven horns** (cf.Matt.28:18; Eph.1:20), and He was given the Holy Spirit to give to His chosen Apostles as symbolized by the **seven eyes** (cf.Jn.14:16-17,26; Acts 2:29-33). This is a pictorial view of the inauguration of Christ as King of kings and Lord of lords. Since Jesus laid claim to all authority in heaven and earth prior to His ascension (Matt.28:18), the scene we are watching took place sometime following Jesus' resurrection and ascension to heaven. This is a pre-Pentecost scene.

The Subjection of Heaven and Earth to the Lamb

Vv. 8-14 When the Lamb took the book worship broke out anew in heaven and on earth. The **living things** and the **Elders** now worshiped and praised the Lamb. This was followed by myriads and myriads of angels, and, finally, the whole creation, worshiping the Lamb. The picture is impressive.

The **living things,** representing the attributes of God, now equally praise the Lamb. The **Elders,** representing the worship of righteous Israel, also praise the Lamb. They worked through faith for the day when the Messiah would reign. Each had **harps** and **golden vials full of odors,** or incense, which represented the prayers of saints. Again, this identifies the elders with the function of priests under the Mosaic era (cf.1 Chron.25:3).

They sang a **new song.** The Lamb's atonement for the sins of the world was offered and accepted and the new order under Christ became a reality. The verse of the song reflects this wonderful change having taken place.

Check several translations on the wording of the song. The original language shows the musical group praising the Lamb for redeeming, or purchasing, **men** for God out of every tribe, language, people and nation. When Jesus died on the cross, He offered one sacrifice for sin forever (Heb.9:28; 10:12). All who would ever be purchased with His blood were purchased with that sacrifice. The song sung at the inauguration of Christ as our King was in anticipation of the worlds' redemption under the New Testament order. All of the redeemed, then, became a kingdom and priests and have reigned with Christ on earth since Pentecost, 30 A.D. (cf.1 Pet.2:5-9).

Next to submit to the Lamb were the angels of heaven. Myriads and myriads of angels praised the Lamb as worthy to receive **power, riches, wisdom, strength, honor, glory, and blessing.** These seven statements of praise indicate the complete worthiness of Christ to receive total praise from God's angels.

The angels were followed by the whole creation likewise praising God and the Lamb. The cycle is complete. All of heaven and earth humbly and equally submit to God and the Lamb (cf.Matt.28:18).

Summary

We have been permitted with John to pictorially view the crowning of Christ as King. He was given **all authority in heaven and in earth** (Matt.28:18). *"Angels and authorities and powers being made subject unto him"* (1 Pet.3:22). Jesus Christ is in control, and we see the throne of God as it exists under the New Testament order to this day.

Home Exercise
Chapter 5

QUESTIONS:

1. Who is the principle character in this chapter? _____
2. Who wept? _____
3. We sing a song similar to one sung in this chapter. What is the title of the song we sing? _____
4. What makes a song new? _____
5. Give another spelling of Juda. _____
6. Who is the one who had the book in his right hand? _____
7. Who is identified as the root of David? _____
8. What symbolizes the prayers of the saints? _____
9. What symbolizes the Holy Spirit? _____
10. List the sevenfold anthem of praise for the Lamb. _____
    _____

TRUE OR FALSE:

1. _____ The scroll in God's right hand was full.
2. _____ The Lamb appeared in order to be slain.
3. _____ The Lamb received equal worship with the Father.
4. _____ No one on earth was worthy to open the book.
5. _____ One of the Elders told John not to weep.
6. _____ The Father handed the scroll to the Lamb.
7. _____ 100,000,000+ angels gathered around God's throne.
8. _____ While men could not open the book they could look upon it.

FILL IN THE BLANKS: **ANSWERS**

1. _____ horns   seven
2. _____ song   root
3. _____ of the tribe of Juda   new
4. _____ angel   kings (kingdom)
5. _____ on the earth   worthy
6. _____ beasts   Lion
7. _____ hand   strong
8. _____ is the Lamb   reign
9. _____ and priests   four
10. _____ vials full of odors   right
11. _____ seals   golden
12. _____ of David

Lesson 10

Chapter 6

The Opening of the First Six Seals

Attention in the remainder of this section (chs 4-11) centers around **the seven seals.** They symbolize the things **shortly to come to pass** in the desolation of the nation of Israel and the destruction of Jerusalem (cf.Lesson 3). When those things were fulfilled, they became the signet of God's approval upon His Word.

Chapter 6 portrays the opening of the first six seals. Remember, John was writing about things **past, present, and future** (1:19). We think the first six seals dealt with the past and present and the seventh dealt with the future things. Only one chapter is given to the first six seals while the seventh commands the attention of four chapters (8-11).

The First Seal

Vv. 1-2 When the Lamb opened the first seal John heard a noise as **thunder,** indicating an approaching storm. One of the **living things** invited the appearance of the first players. A **white horse** appeared.[10] The rider of the white horse had a bow in his hand and was given a crown (the ***stephanos,*** the victor's crown). He was groomed for his position, and went forth "as a conqueror bent on conquest" (NIV).

This horse and rider represent the development of the kingdom foretold by Daniel through which the holy people (Israel) would be destroyed and scattered (Dan.7,8,9,12). The Roman Empire was the kingdom by which these things were accomplished. Daniel pictures the transformation from the Roman Republic to the Empire under the Caesars (Dan.7).

---

[10] Hailey, Homer, *A Commentary On The Minor Prophets,* (Grand Rapids, Baker Book House, 1972), page 348. "White is the festive color, or color of victory."

The Second Seal

Vv. 3-4   Another **living thing** invited the
appearance of the second horse and rider. This
horse was **red.** The rider had power to take peace
from the earth with his great sword. Red is
thought to symbolize **bloodshed.**

This horse and rider represent the Red Army
of Rome which marched through the world killing
foes and subduing nations. They subjected the
world to the wishes of Rome, took away the will of
the people, destroying the peace. Civil war erupted in many
quarters, particularly in Judea.

The Third Seal

 **Vv. 5-6**   A third **living thing** invited the
appearance of the third horse and rider. This
horse was **black** and the rider had a pair of scales
in his hand. A voice from the midst of the four
living things says, *"A measure of wheat for a*
penny, and three measures of barley for a
penny; and see thou hurt not the oil and the
wine."

This horse and rider symbolize gloom, distress, despair, want,
famine, etc. The scales indicate food shortages with high prices
demanded for what was available. The Romans possessed the
ability to create these conditions by besieging cities, cutting off
incoming supplies. Such was the end to which Jerusalem came.
The cry to spare the **oil and wine** was designed to guarantee the
continuation of the daily sacrifices in the Jewish Temple. The daily
sacrifices were accompanied by these commodities. Josephus
confirms their use until just before the Temple was destroyed.

The Fourth Seal

Vv. 7-8 A pale horse appeared with the opening of the
fourth seal. The rider was named **death,** and **Hades**
followed. He had power over a fourth part of earth to
kill with **sword, hunger, death,** and **beasts.**

The color of this horse was a sick green
symbolizing death. The rider was named **Death** to
symbolize the powers by which death came to the
Jews. Some died by the sword, others by starvation,
diseases and other plagues of war, and others by beasts
in the theaters.

The Fifth Seal

Vv. 9-11 When the fifth seal was opened John saw the altar (of burnt offering) with the souls of martyred saints under it. They were crying for vengeance. They were given white robes and told to continue their rests until others were likewise martyred for their faith.

Who are these martyred saints? Our clues identify them as Old Testament saints. (1) They were under the altar which associates them with Old Testament worship. (2) They were given white robes (cf.7:14). Since they were dead before receiving white robes, they must be identified as Old Testament saints (Heb.9:15; 10:12). (3) They were to continue resting until their fellow-servants and brethren were also martyred (cf.Lk.11:46-51). (4) When this Apocalypse ends, **God's servants the prophets** had been avenged (11:18).

The Sixth Seal

Vv. 12-17 The opening of the sixth seal was followed by a great earthquake, the sun being darkened and the moon becoming as blood. The heaven was rolled together as a scroll with distress and fear everywhere. Some cried for the mountains and rocks to fall on them because of the severity of the wrath of God.

The language compares to Jesus' discourse describing **the great tribulation** which preceded the destruction of Jerusalem (Matt.24, Mk.13; Lk.21:5-32). The **earthquake** symbolized the shaking up of the nation. The closing of the scroll, darkening of the sun and moon, falling of the stars, and the moving of mountains and islands symbolize God's closing the book and turning out the lights on the nation of Israel. This judgment was so severe the people cried for the mountains and rocks to fall on them (Lk.23:28-31).

Home Exercise
Chapter 6

QUESTIONS:

1. Who was in charge of opening the seals? _____

2. What is the principle question of this chapter? _____

3. What reason was given why some would call for the mountains
   and rocks to fall on them? _____

4. Why were the martyrs under the altar slain? _____

5. Explain the difference between DEATH and HELL: _____
   _____

TRUE OR FALSE:

1. _____ White is thought to symbolize **mourning.**
2. _____ Red is thought to symbolize **bloodshed.**
3. _____ Black is thought to be the **festive** color.
4. _____ Pale symbolizes **sickness, disease, death.**
5. _____ White robes were given to those cleansed in the
         blood of Christ. (cf.7:14)
6. _____ The moon will someday turn to blood.
7. _____ The stars can literally fall to earth.
8. _____ Oil and wine were used in the sacrifices.
9. _____ The Lamb also pours out His wrath.
10. _____ The text states the martyrs were slain for **the
          testimony of Jesus.**

MATCH TO THE PROPER SEAL:

1. _____ earthquake	11. _____ scarcity
2. _____ scales	12. _____ a conqueror
3. _____ beasts of earth	13. _____ war
4. _____ a bow	14. _____ a shake up
5. _____ the altar	15. _____ martyrs
6. _____ great sword	16. _____ rest
7. _____ a fig tree	17. _____ Hades
8. _____ farm products	18. _____ a crown
9. _____ fellow-servants	19. _____ nobles
10. _____ a scroll	20. _____ vengeance

Lesson 11

Chapter 7

The First Interlude

Prelude

The first six seals set the stage for the final one. The forces of destruction by which God would carry out His purposes against Israel are represented by the first four seals. The fifth seal portrayed Old Testament prophets and saints, slain by Israel, crying for vengeance. The sixth seal focused upon **the great tribulation** foretold by Jesus and the prophets. We are now ready to observe the opening of the seventh seal in which the things determined upon Israel are carried out. Before viewing it, however, we must understand that God's plan for redeeming the world is at work accomplishing His purpose. Chapter 7 is an interlude between the sixth and seventh seal designed to reveal this information.

The Restraining of the Four Winds

V. 1 John saw four angels standing on the four corners of earth holding back the four winds so they could not blow upon the earth, sea or any tree. The winds were ready to unleash their power when the time appointed was ready.

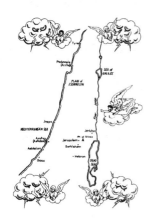

The four winds represent the storm winds which were brewing. The winds blow from the four corners of earth; i.e., northeast, southwest, etc. John's use of the winds was to picture an impending storm on the horizon. Since the power of destruction upon Israel was the Roman Empire, the four winds represent the destructive forces of the empire. These forces are first seen in the first four seals. When the storm was over and the saints avenged, the destruction was accomplished through **the kingdoms of the world** (11:15).

The Angel with the Seal of God

Vv. 2-3 John next observed another angel ascending from the East with the seal of God. He cried with a loud voice to the four angels holding the four winds not to hurt the earth, sea, or any trees, until God's servants were sealed in their foreheads.

Jesus alone has the power to seal God's servants (Jn.14:6; Acts 4:12; Rev.3:12), so this angel represents the spirit of Christ in sealing God's servants. The seal of God is His signet of approval. The sealed servant belongs to God.

The Sealing of the 144,000

Vv. 4-8 John heard the number of the sealed. There were **144,000** out of **all** the tribes of Israel. John named twelve tribes assigning 12,000 sealed saints to each tribe to reach the magic number.

Who are they? John tells and we must listen to the clues he gives. He says they are from **all the tribes of the children of Israel.** If nothing else was known, this should be enough to identify them.

John saw the 144,000 again in chapter 14 standing with the Lamb on Mount Zion already sealed. They are identified as **the first-fruits unto God and the Lamb** (14:4). This distinguishes them as Old Testament saints because the first-fruits purchased unto God and the Lamb with the blood of Christ were the Old Testament saints (Heb.9:15; 12:23).

The 144,000 represent the saved of Israel from under the Mosaic covenant. The number was complete and will never change because no others will ever be saved under that covenant. It is not literal but symbolic of the total number saved under the Law. The scene in chapter 7 must be viewed taking place after the resurrection of Christ and before Pentecost.

The Innumerable Multitude

Vv. 9-14 Next, John saw an innumerable multitude from all nations, kindreds, people and tongues standing before the Lamb clothed in white with palms in their hands. They praised God and the Lamb as the angels join saying, *"Amen: Blessing, and glory, and wisdom, and thanksgiving, and honor, and power, and might, be unto our God for ever and ever. Amen."* John was then informed that this multitude was made up of those coming out of **the great tribulation** having washed their robes in the blood of the Lamb.

This multitude cannot be numbered because they continued coming out of the tribulation.[11] They were coming from among all the nations which identifies them with New Testament saints. We learn later that they were also sealed in their foreheads (cf.22:4).

These are they that come out of the great tribulation (ASV). This was a specific period of tribulation (cf.Jer.30:7-9; Dan.12:1; Matt.24:21). Since the period of tribulation preceding the destruction of Jerusalem was to be greater than any before or after, it must of necessity be **the great tribulation** referred to in this text.

Josephus reported how difficult conditions became for the Jews before Jerusalem was destroyed in 70 A.D. He said, *"It appears to me that the misfortunes of all men, from the beginning of the world, if they be compared to these of the Jews, are not so considerable as they were."*[12] A conflict developed between the Jews and the nations of the world under Roman rule that was a disaster to many, many thousands of people both Jews and Gentiles. The indiscriminate taking of life in this conflict would have claimed the lives of many Christians. These are the saints John saw coming out of the great tribulation.

The remaining verses of the chapter associate the saints in their spiritual relationship with the Lamb as the same relationship described in chapters 21-22. We will discuss them more fully when we get to those chapters. It will be helpful, however, to note that the characteristics of new Jerusalem are viewed as a present reality when John saw the Apocalypse.

---

[11] Hailey, Homer, *Commentary on Revelation*, (Grand Rapids, Baker Book House, 1979), page 209.

[12] Josephus, *The Wars of the Jews*, Preface, 4.

Home Exercise
Chapter 7

MATCHING:

1.	_____ Place where sealed	a.	12,000
2.	_____ 12,000	b.	from the east
3.	_____ blood of the lamb	c.	the four winds
4.	_____ innumerable multitude	d.	God
5.	_____ midst of the throne	e.	forehead
6.	_____ worshiped God	f.	the Lamb
7.	_____ 144,000 sealed	g.	in their hands
8.	_____ angel ascended	h.	out of all nations
9.	_____ at 4 corners of earth	i.	in his temple
10.	_____ Reuben	j.	Gad
11.	_____ palms	k.	angels stood
12.	_____ angels held back	l.	of 12 tribes of Israel
13.	_____ great	m.	angels
14.	_____ place of service	n.	tribulation
15.	_____ to wipe away tears	o.	white robes

FILL IN THE BLANKS:

1. "_____ angels standing on the _____ _____ of the earth, holding the _____ winds of the earth, that the wind should not _____ on the earth, nor on the _____, nor on any _____."
2. "I saw another angel _____ from the _____, having the _____ of the _____ God."
3. He cried to the _____ _____ holding the four _____ not to _____ the "earth, neither the _____, nor the _____, till we have _____ the servants of our God in their _____."
4. The great innumerable _____ cried saying, "_____ to our _____..., and unto the _____."

MULTIPLE CHOICE:

1. The tribe of (Dan; Levi; Gad) is not usually mentioned as one of the twelve tribes of Israel.
2. In 7:12 (majesty; glory; thanksgiving) replaces riches in the sevenfold anthem of 5:12.
3. The Lamb will lead his servants to (be sealed; praise God; living fountains of water).
4. God is pictured as wiping away (all tears; sweat; sins) of his servants.

Lesson 12

Chapter 8

Seventh Seal; First Four Trumpets

The first six seals bring us into the tribulation period. The seventh will carry us through the Roman-Jewish war to the end–the final destruction of Jerusalem. The seventh seal covers chapters 8-11.

Heaven's Reaction

Vv. 1-2 When the seventh seal was opened, there was silence in heaven for half an hour after which John saw seven angels standing before God with seven trumpets.

God's judgment was about to be executed against Israel and it was time for solemn reflection (Hab.2:20). The events being revealed involved judgments with grave consequences. Even the heavens were awed at the prospect of what was about to happen.

Seven trumpeting angels, ready to open the curtains on the unfolding scenes, appear. Their trumpets symbolize **the alarm of war** (Jer.4:19).

The Prayers of Saints Ascend

Vv. 3-5 Another angel appeared at the altar. He had a golden censer and much incense to offer with the prayers of all saints upon the golden altar (cf.altar of incense in the Jewish Temple). The smoke of the incense was mixed with the prayers of **all saints** and ascended into God's presence. Fire from the altar was then placed in the censer and cast into the earth.

The scene is designed to symbolize the presence of the prayers of suffering saints before God. The prayers of Old Testament saints were joined with those of the New Testament. The prayers were heard and answered. Fire, taken from the altar (burnt offering, cf.Lev.16:12-13; 10:1-2), was placed in the censer and cast into the earth symbolizing the kindling of the fires of passion which lead to the ultimate end of the nation of Israel.

Introduction to the Trumpets

Reading Josephus' account of the Roman-Jewish war is helpful in understanding this section. His treatment of the war's chronological development reveals the same order as presented in the Apocalypse.

The war began this way. General Vespasian, upon being ordered by Emperor Nero into Syria, moved with haste gathering an army of 60,000 to subdue the Jews. Meanwhile, the Jews, aware of the consequences of their rebellion against the Romans, also assembled an army of 60,000 under General Josephus. The Jews made Galilee their first line of defense. All of the early battles in the war were fought in Galilee.

The First Trumpet

Vv. 6-7 When the first trumpeting angel sounded, **hail and fire mingled with blood** were cast upon the earth (land) and a third part of the trees and all of the grass were burned up.

Hail symbolizes implements of war (cf.Ezek.13:11-16). The Romans using machines for throwing arrows, darts and stones invaded Galilee resulting in **fire mingled with blood.**[13] The four winds, restrained from hurting the earth (land), sea and trees (7:1-2), were released. Vespasian quickly subdued Galilee bringing them into submission to Rome.

The Second Trumpet

Vv. 8-9 When the second angel sounded, John saw as it were a great mountain burning cast into the sea. A third part of the creatures with life died, and a third part of the ships were destroyed and a third part of the sea became blood.

The winds now hurt the sea. This scene depicts disaster for the Jews upon the sea. **Mountains** symbolize world powers and in this text identify the Romans (cf.Jer.51:25). The **creatures with life** are human beings, and the **ships**

---

[13] Josephus, *Wars*, 3,5,2; 3,4,1.

identify the vessels in which the creatures were found. Josephus reports the disastrous attempts of the Jews to fight upon the seas.[14]

The Third Trumpet

Vv. 10-11 The third angel sounded and a great burning star called Wormwood fell upon a third part of the rivers and the fountains of waters making them bitter. Many men died as a result.

A falling star symbolizes the fall of a dignitary. This star fell upon the waters which symbolize people (17:5). The **rivers** are the channels though which the waters flow from the fountains or sources of waters. Jerusalem was the capital of the nation of Israel and the fountain from which the life, law, religion, authority, etc., of the Jews flowed. When their great commander surrendered in Galilee, the conditions described in this scene occurred.[15]

The Fourth Trumpet

Vv. 12-13 One third of the sun, moon and stars was darkened when the fourth angel sounded. This was followed by an **eagle** flying through heaven warning of the terrible judgments yet to come.

We learned previously that the darkening of the sun, moon and stars means God's light is going out on a nation. When Galilee fell to the Romans, one third of the nation of Israel was conquered and is pictured in this scene. At this point in the war, Emperor Nero died, and General Vespasian withdrew his troops from the war. The eagle flying through heaven corresponds to this respite in the war and warned that the worst was yet to come.

---

[14] *Ibid.*, 3,9,2-3; 3,10,9.

[15] *Ibid.*, 3,9,5-6.

Home Exercise
Chapter 8

QUESTIONS:

1. Who opened the seventh seal? _____

2. What part of the Mosaic Tabernacle corresponds to the golden altar? _____

3. What happened when the seventh seal was opened? _____

4. How many angels are identified in chapter 8? _____

5. What part of the things mentioned are affected by the first four trumpets? _____

MATCHING:

1. _____ Wormwood   a. Seven angels
2. _____ An eagle (KJV angel) b. sea
3. _____ Angel at altar   c. blood
4. _____ A great star fell   d. ships destroyed
5. _____ Cast into the sea   e. Much incense
6. _____ Sun, Moon, Stars   f. burned up
7. _____ Hail, Fire   g. a great mountain
8. _____ Seven trumpets   h. bitter
9. _____ Prayers of saints   i. burning as a lamp
10. _____ Blood   j. golden censer
11. _____ Trees and grass   k. flying
12. _____ 2nd Trumpeting angel l. smitten

COMPARE THE FOLLOWING TEXTS AND EXPLAIN:

1. Compare the altar in Revelation 6:9 to that described in 8:3-5. Are they the same? _____

2. Explain how the things forbidden to be hurt in 7:3 are hurt in 8:7. _____

3. Compare the language of 6:12-13 with 8:12 and explain the differences, if any. _____

4. Compare Revelation 4:5 with 8:5 and explain the difference, if any. _____

Lesson 13
Chapter 9

The Fifth and Sixth Trumpets

The first four trumpeting angels symbolize the first half of the Roman-Jewish war. The first trumpet symbolized the war in Galilee. The second symbolized the war upon the sea. The third signified the fall of a dignitary causing strife, and the fourth, the subjection of one third of the nation. An eagle flying through heaven warns of three remaining **woes.**

At this point in the war, Emperor Nero died and Vespasian ceased his conquest of the Jews for about a year and a half while awaiting orders from the new government. When orders did not come, Vespasian sent an army to Rome, claiming the throne for himself. He then sent his son, Titus, back to Palestine to conclude the war. The second half of the war, and the opposing sides who fought in the war, are symbolized by the fifth and sixth trumpets.

The Fifth Trumpet, The First Woe

 **Vv. 1-12** Many things happened when the fifth angel sounded. A **fallen star** opened **the bottomless pit** (abyss) and billowing smoke arose darkening the sun and polluting the air. Out of the smoke came **locusts** to hurt those men who were not the servants of God. They were permitted to torment men five months. The torment would be so severe men would seek death and it would flee from them. The locusts were shaped like horses with crowns of gold on their heads and faces like men. They had hair like women, teeth like lions, breastplates of iron, and tails like scorpions. They sounded like chariots of many horses running to battle. Their king was the angel of the **abyss** and was called **Abaddon** in Hebrew and **Apollyon** in Greek.

The fallen star (**angel**) is Satan. He had already fallen when John saw him (cf.Lk.10:18; Jn.12:31; Rev.12:9). The **abyss** is the abode of demons (Lk.8:31). The smoke arising from the abyss is symbolic of Satan's evil influence in the war. The smoke pollutes the air and out of this polluted atmosphere comes a plague of locusts to destroy men.

All of this symbolizes the foul tempers that possessed the Jews during the last stages of the Roman-Jewish war. When Galilee fell, three warring zealot factions converged on Jerusalem with thousands of supporters. Though warring among themselves, they agreed to fight together against the Romans. Of these warring factions Josephus says, ***"They brought the Hebrew nation into contempt... They confessed what was true, that they were the slaves, the scum, and the spurious and abortive offspring of our nation."***[16]

These locusts warriors were to hurt only wicked men. Christians would have obeyed the Lord's instructions and vacated Jerusalem by this point in the war (cf.Lk.21:20-21).[17] The torment of the locusts would continue five months. The other identifying expressions were designed to magnify this wicked Jewish force as a powerful foe for the Romans.[18] Satan was their King. The suffering of the Jews in Jerusalem from these wicked zealots was beyond our imagination.

The Sixth Trumpet, The Second Woe

Vv. 13-21 When the sixth angel sounded, a voice from the horns of the golden altar commanded the loosing of four angels bound in Euphrates. They were prepared for the hour to slay the third part of men. The army numbered 200,000,000. The warriors had breastplates of fire, jacinth and brimstone. Their horses had heads of lions with fire, smoke and brimstone issuing out of their mouths. They kill a third part of men. They had power in their mouths and tails. Their tails were like serpents with heads which hurt when they strike, and they unleashed their power against a group of wicked men too stubborn to repent.

---

[16] Josephus, *Wars*, 5,10,5.

[17] Ogden, Arthur M., *The Avenging of the Apostles and Prophets* (Ogden Publications, 1985) page 67.

[18] Josephus makes many statements about the seditious Jews which help to explain John's language. You would do well to read them: Josephus, *Wars*, 4,6,3; 4,9,3-12; 5,1,5; 5,2,5; 5,9,2.

The Roman side of the war is being developed. It came in response to the prayers of saints offered on the golden altar. God heard and answered their prayers.

The loosing of the four angels bound at Euphrates symbolizes the determination of the Romans to finish the destruction of Jerusalem. When Vespasian ordered Titus back to Palestine to conclude the war against the Jews, Titus returned to Cesarea where he gathered an army of 80,000 men. Among this number were Rome's finest soldiers, the border guards protecting the Empire's eastern border along the river Euphrates. While the army was only 80,000 strong, they represented the rest of the world estimated at that time at 200,000,000.

"Their breastplates were fiery red, dark blue, and yellow as sulfur" (NIV). This may symbolize the colors of the Roman armor and that of the other kings, or it may tell us that these forces were the instruments of divine judgment being carried out. The horses issue fire, smoke and brimstone out of their mouths which are symbols of divine judgment (cf.Gen.19:24; Psa.18:7-9; Jer.15:14). When Jesus described His coming in judgment, He said, *"But the same day that Lot went out of Sodom it rained fire and brimstone from heaven, and destroyed them all.* ***Even thus shall it be in the day when the Son of man is revealed"*** (Lk.17:29-30).

The final two verses deal with the results. The Jewish zealots, who were guilty of all these sins, did not repent when confronted by the Romans.[19] Though they were given many opportunities to repent, they only mocked the Romans. Apparently, there has never been a more wicked, shameful and disgraceful bunch of human scum ever to walk upon earth. **God poured upon them the fullness of His wrath!**

---

[19] *Ibid.,* 5,9,3-6; 6,6,2; 5,12,4; 5,13,7.

Home Exercise
Chapter 9

TRUE OR FALSE:

1. _____ The river Euphrates is found in South America.
2. _____ A scorpion is a termite that stings like a bee.
3. _____ The locusts were to eat everything in sight.
4. _____ Only God's servants would escape their torment.
5. _____ The locusts plague would last only five months.
6. _____ The locusts were shaped like men and had faces like horses.
7. _____ The golden altar had four horns.
8. _____ Horses were seen with heads like lions.
9. _____ Tails are seen that are like scorpion heads.
10. _____ Those punished by the woes speedily repented.

FILL IN THE BLANKS:

1. A third part of men were killed by horses who breathed out _____, _____, and _____.
2. The locusts warriors had _____ as of iron and made a noise that sounded like _____ of _____ running to battle.
3. Those punished are said to have worshiped idols of _____, _____, _____, _____, and _____ which could not _____, _____, or _____.
4. They were punished because they would not repent of their _____, _____, _____, _____, and _____.

MATCHING:

1. _____ Key to bottomless pit
2. _____ Angel of bottomless pit
3. _____ Jacinth and brimstone
4. _____ 200 thousand
5. _____ Four bound angels
6. _____ Hebrew for name
7. _____ Came out of the smoke
8. _____ Darkened by the smoke
9. _____ Greek for name

a. breastplates of fire
b. Abaddon
c. Apollyon
d. Locusts
e. The fallen star
f. Was King
g. loosed
h. sun and air
i. an army

Lesson 14

Chapter 10

The Second Interlude

The stage has been set for the finale of this apocalyptic vision. The sides that meet head-on in the great battle of the day of God's wrath have been introduced. We are now ready for the things determined by God to be fulfilled. Before this happens, however, an interlude is inserted to explain all elements at work in this operation. We must understand clearly what happens in this symbolic picture.

The Mighty Angel With the Little Book

Vv. 1-2 John saw another mighty angel come down from heaven clothed with a cloud and a rainbow upon his head. His face was shining as the sun. His feet, the right one upon the sea and the left upon the earth, were as pillars of fire. He had a little book opened in his hand.

Who is this mighty angel? We are not told but, evidently, he represents the Son of God. He was clothed with a cloud symbolic of his coming in the clouds (cf.1:7). The rainbow upon his head symbolizes his relationship to God's throne (cf.4:3). His face and feet associate him with the vision personage of chapter 1 (cf.1:15-16). His feet upon the sea and land signify his universal authority, and the little book portrays the New Testament as the power by which He rules (Matt.28:18). Though some question our identity of Him as the Son of God, we feel that Jesus' position as God's special messenger to mankind qualifies Him to be represented by this mighty angel. The scene pictures Him ruling with all authority through the power of the little book and ready to complete God's judgment upon Israel (Matt.24:30; 26:24).

The Seven Thunders

Vv. 3-4 Next, John heard him speak in a loud, lion-like, voice followed by the voices of **seven thunders.** John was forbidden to write about them and we cannot speculate. **Thunder** symbolizes an approaching storm. The seven thunders placed at this juncture in the Apocalypse indicates that the full fury of God's storm upon Israel was about to be unleashed.

The Oath

Vv. 5-7 The mighty angel swore by the God of all creation that there would be no longer delay. The sounding of the seventh trumpet would signal the finishing of the mystery of God declared to his servants the prophets.

"There should be time no longer" (KJV) should be understood *"there will be no more delay"* (NIV).[20] The vengeance sought had been delayed. The martyred Old Testament saints rested until their fellow-servants and brethren were also tried and slain (6:11). Now, everything was ready for their blood to be avenged. There would be no longer delay.

The blowing of the seventh trumpet would signify the end and establish the finishing of the mystery of God. The mystery identifies the New Testament order.[21] It was revealed in a mystery in the Old Testament by **God's servants the prophets.** It would be **finished,** i.e., performed, accomplished, executed, or fulfilled.[22] In other words, all prophecies concerning the messiah, his kingdom, and the New Testament order would be accomplished by Jerusalem's destruction in 70 A.D. Other passages teach the same thing (cf.Dan.9:24-27; Lk.21:22).

Jesus said, *"For these be the days of vengeance, that all things which are written may be fulfilled"* (Lk.21:22). Jesus was discussing the destruction of Jerusalem when He spoke these words. *"All things which are written"* means the same as *"the mystery... declared to his servants the prophets"* (Rev.10:7). The New Testament was not written when Jesus spoke as recorded in Luke, therefore, the Old Testament scriptures were being fulfilled in the destruction of Jerusalem. If all of the Old Testament scriptures were fulfilled by or in the destruction of Jerusalem, the mystery of God of necessity had to be finished by or

---

[20] Check your translations. Most agree the text should read, *"there shall be no longer delay."*

[21] See discussion in Lesson 4 page 15 of the Introduction.

[22] Cf. Thayer, *TELEO*, page 619.

at the same time. A study of the context of each passage will show they are discussing the same subject matter.[23]

John's Commission to Eat the Book

Vv. 8-10 John was instructed by the voice from heaven to take the little book from the hand of the angel and eat it. It would make his belly bitter and his mouth sweet as honey. So, John took the book, ate it, and his mouth was sweet and his belly bitter.

Assuming the little book symbolizes the New Testament we can understand why it was sweet to his mouth. It contains the sweet message of God's saving grace promised to all. Sweeter blessings have never been afforded mankind. The little book was also bitter because the same book, which brings the good news of salvation, also contains the promises of destruction upon the nation (Israel) through whom our Savior came into the world. They rejected their Messiah and sealed their doom. To John, as a loyal Jew, this message was bitter.

The Promise

Vv. 11 In the closing verse, John was promised he would prophesy again before many people. This would have been very unlikely at John's advanced age if he wrote the Apocalypse in 95 or 96 A.D. This promise better fits the earlier dating of Revelation.

---

[23] Ogden, Arthur M., *The Avenging of the Apostles and Prophets* (Ogden Publications, 1985) pages 17-19, 246-247.

Home Exercise
Chapter 10

MATCHING:

1. _____ bitter	a. eat it up
2. _____ mouth	b. a lion
3. _____ pillars of fire	c. his face
4. _____ Write them not	d. God's servants
5. _____ the prophets	e. belly
6. _____ clothed with cloud	f. his right foot
7. _____ open	g. his feet
8. _____ roareth	h. the 7 thunders
9. _____ the sun	i. a mighty angel
10. _____ take it	j. rainbow
11. _____ upon his head	k. little book
12. _____ upon the sea	l. sweet

MULTIPLE CHOICE:

1. We associate **thunder** with (sunny skies; a storm; a cloudy day).
2. John was told to (ignore; record; seal up) the seven thunders.
3. John was to (burn; read; eat) the book.
4. John was told he would (prophesy; die; be translated).
5. John saw the mighty angel (set the islands on fire; overthrow Satan; swear by heaven).
6. The (fifth; sixth; seventh) trumpeting angel is mentioned in this chapter.
7. The (mystery of God; life on earth; the law of Moses) was finished when the seventh trumpet was sounded.
8. The mystery of God had been declared to (us; kings; the prophets).

TRUE OR FALSE:

1. _____ The little book had seven seals upon it.
2. _____ The seven thunders symbolize a ferocious storm about to be unleashed.
3. _____ John fully explained the seven thunders.
4. _____ Old Testament prophets are called **"God's servants the prophets."**
5. _____ John was told he would prophecy again.
6. _____ John ate something that made him sick.

Lesson 15
Chapter 11

The Seventh Trumpet, The Final Woe
The Measuring of the Temple

Vv. 1-2 The interlude continues: John was given a reed like a rod and commanded to measure the temple, the altar and the worshipers. He was not to measure the court outside the temple or the Holy City for they were given to the Gentiles to tread under foot forty-two months.

The reed was a measuring stick (cf.Ezek.40:3). It was like a rod to symbolize the measuring of the city for punishment (cf.Prov.13:24; 22:15; 23:13; 1 Cor.4:21). When new Jerusalem was measured for preservation, a golden reed was used (21:15-16).

This was a visionary measuring of **Jerusalem,** the **Holy City,** where the **temple of God** was located, and *"where also our Lord was crucified"* (11:8). How can we doubt this conclusion? Further, it is said the Gentiles would tread her under foot 42 months. Jesus used these very words during his personal ministry when discussing Jerusalem's destruction (cf.Lk.21:24). The Roman war against the Jews began in early spring, 67 A.D., and concluded in late summer, 70 A.D., forty-two months later.

The Two Witnesses

Vv. 3-12 The angel promised power for his two witnesses to prophesy 1260 days. The witnesses were the two olive trees and candlesticks (lampstands) standing before God. They had power to hurt men with fire proceeding out of their mouths, to turn water to blood, smite the earth with plagues and stop the rain. They were to be killed by the beast out of the abyss, and their bodies lie in the street of the great city, spiritually called Sodom and Egypt, where also our Lord was crucified. They would not be permitted burial. Those who dwelt on the earth would rejoice at their death because they were tormented by these prophets. After three and a half days they would be resurrected and called up to heaven in the presence of their enemies.

Identifying the two witnesses will be helpful. The olive trees and lampstands symbolize the sources of spiritual light to the Jews, the **law and the prophets.** Moses was the giver of the law (Jn.1:17), and Elijah was the beginning of the prophets used by God to warn Israel and call them to repentance. When men rejected Moses' and Elijah's testimony, fire from God destroyed them (cf.Moses, Num.11:1-4; 16:23-35; Elijah, 1 Kings 18; 2 Kings 1:5-17). Moses also had power to turn water to blood and smite the earth with plagues (Ex.4-12; Deut.28:58-68), and Elijah had power to withhold the rain (1 Kings 17:1-7; Jas.5:17-18). The two witnesses were Moses and Elijah who represent the law and the prophets. They continued testifying to the Jews through the teaching and practice of the Old Testament Scriptures during the

war until just before Jerusalem fell, when worship in the Temple ceased.

The two witnesses were killed by the beast ascending out of the abyss. This beast does not appear until chapter 13 (cf.17:7-8). It symbolizes the Roman Empire which destroyed Jerusalem. The Roman siege of Jerusalem ultimately ended the teaching and practice of the law and the prophets thus symbolically putting them to death. The nations rejoiced because the teaching and practice of the law and the prophets, which had tormented them, ceased.

They were resurrected after three and one half days to symbolize the fulfillment of their prophecies. As we pointed out in our studies (cf.Lesson 4, pages 16-18), they foretold the end, **the latter end** of the nation. When the temple in Jerusalem was burned, it verified the accuracy of their testimony. Thus vindicated, they ascended to heaven in complete triumph and fulfillment as their enemies observed. God, who ordered and directed them, brought them back to His throne symbolizing the end of their earthly use. With the destruction of the temple, their practice ended.

The Fall of One Tenth of the City

Vv. 13-14 The same hour there was a great earthquake and a tenth part of the city fell. Seven thousand were slain and the rest frightened. They gave glory to God. The second woe passed.

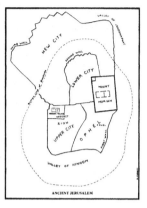

ANCIENT JERUSALEM

The probable reference here is to the fall of the temple mount in Jerusalem. A map of the ancient city shows that the temple area occupied about a tenth of Jerusalem. Josephus reported 10,000 killed when the temple area fell to the Romans. John's figure symbolizes the total number killed in the fall of the temple. Josephus' number is an estimate.

The Final Trumpet, Heaven Rejoices

Vv. 15-19 The seventh angel sounded and great voices in heaven began praising God for using the kingdoms of men to demonstrate His reign. The twenty-four elders also praised God in worship because He had demonstrated His reign. Then they explain that all of this happened in order to reward **God's servants the prophets,** the saints, and all that feared God's name. This was followed by God's new temple being opened in heaven wherein was found the ark of his testament.

The context clearly shows that our picture is of God using the kingdoms of men to accomplish His purpose. He did so to demonstrate His reign and to avenge the blood of His servants. The avenging of His servants the prophets clearly show that this judgment was upon Jerusalem as He had amply foretold.

Conclusion

With this chapter we conclude this division of the book, **The Heavenly Apocalypse.** We observed the exaltation of Christ to God's throne and viewed an orderly presentation of God avenging His persecuted people. Our faith should be stronger realizing the Apocalypse is not a mass of unintelligible absurdities, but an orderly presentation of God's throne working in behalf of His people.

Home Exercise
Chapter 11

QUESTIONS:

1. How long is *"a thousand two hundred and threescore days"* in days? _____ Months? _____ Years? _____
2. What is the name of the only city in the Bible called **"the holy city?"** _____
3. Why was it called **the holy city?** _____
4. What comes from olives that is used for light? _____
5. Who in the Old Testament used God's power to stop it from raining? _____
6. Who used the power God gave them to turn water into blood and smite the earth with plagues? _____
7. Who is said would kill God's two witnesses? _____
8. Where was our Lord crucified? _____
9. How did God and Christ demonstrate their reign? _____
10. What Old Testament group was given reward? _____

MATCH EACH TO THEIR PURPOSE:

1. _____ 24 elders	a.	and the worshipers
2. _____ beast from abyss	b.	ascended to heaven
3. _____ reed	c.	tread upon holy city
4. _____ two witnesses	d.	tenth part of city fell
5. _____ temple, altar	e.	testified
6. _____ the Gentiles	f.	worshiped God
7. _____ the street	g.	to measure the temple
8. _____ angry nations	h.	war against witnesses
9. _____ witnesses raised	i.	thy wrath is come
10. _____ great earthquake	j.	dead bodies in it

FILL IN THE BLANKS:

1. John was not permitted to measure the _____ without because it and the _____ _____ were given to the _____ to _____ under foot.
2. _____ would come out of the mouths of the two witnesses if any man _____ them.
3. *"The kingdoms of this world are become the _____ of our Lord, and of His _____; and He shall reign for _____ and _____."*

Lesson 16

Chapter 12

The Underlying Conflict

Introduction

We are now ready for the third division of Revelation, **The Earthly Apocalypse** (chapters 12-20). Here the emphasis is upon the earthly instruments used in carrying out the desolation of Israel and the destruction of Jerusalem. Once this day of wrath is completed, a conflict develops between the Lamb and the instruments He used. Finally, those instruments are destroyed and the Lamb and His saints reign victoriously.

Chapter 12 develops the undercurrent at work in the events being revealed. The conflict with Israel is only a part of the deeper struggle between good and evil, righteousness and sin, Christ and Satan. The battle raged until Satan was defeated and cast out of his spiritual domain into earth where he persecuted God's people.

The Glorious Woman and The Red Dragon

Vv. 1-4 Two great wonders appeared. The first was a pregnant woman clothed with the sun, the moon under her feet and a crown of twelve stars on her head. She was about to give birth to a boy. Standing before her was a great red dragon with seven crowned heads and ten horns ready to devour her child as soon as he was born. His tail drew a third of the stars of heaven which he cast into the earth.

The **red dragon** represents **Satan** (v.9). But who is this woman? Some say, "Mary"; others, "The church." Two clues assist in reaching a conclusion: (1) Her son and (2) her adversary, Satan, the serpent. When the conflict over Satan and sin developed in the

Garden of Eden, God cursed Satan saying, *"I will put enmity between thee and the woman, and between thy seed and her seed; it shall bruise thy head, and thou shalt bruise his heal"* (Gen.3:15). The picture before us in Revelation portrays that conflict.

Though Mary carried Jesus into the world, she was not the woman. This woman shined brightly as she bore a relationship to the moon and wore a crown of twelve stars. The vision was designed to depict the lineage through which Christ came; the holy seed of the nation of Israel included.[24] Israel's relationship to the moon and to the twelve patriarchs is symbolized. Perhaps the picture is more vivid when Isaiah pictured this spiritual and righteous Israel being delivered of the man child. Afterward, the earth brought forth, and the new, different Jerusalem emerged (Isa.66:5-24).

The Man Child

Vv. 5-6 The child was born and caught up to the throne of God to rule all nations with a rod of iron. The woman then fled to a place prepared in the wilderness where she would be feed 1260 days.

God foretold the birth of this man child (Isa.66:7-8) who would rule with the rod of iron (Psa.2:6-9). It is Christ, the Messiah. Here, again, He is portrayed in heaven with God on His throne. A review of chapter five is in order.

The Spiritual War

Vv. 7-9 War in heaven broke out. Michael and his angels fought against Satan and his angels. Satan and his angels were cast out.

This is the spiritual war promised in Genesis 3:15. Satan tried devouring the woman's seed but failed. Christ was bruised by the attempt but His subsequent resurrection and ascension to heaven marked the attempt as failure. The blood of Christ provided for man remission of sins and redemption, thus signifying the defeat of Satan. He had ruled all men through sin (Rom.3:23). In this sense, Satan had authority in heaven. With God's acceptance of the atonement, Satan no longer ruled. He was cast out into the earth because now he must conquer and rule men before they die.

---

[24] For a full discussion of this woman see *The Avenging of the Apostles and Prophets*, Ogden, pages 266-270. Also see Hailey's *Commentary on Revelation*, pages 368-369.

Rejoicing in Heaven

Vv. 10-11 John heard a voice in heaven declaring that salvation, strength, the kingdom of God and the power of Christ had now come because Satan was cast out. Those rejoicing had gained their victory through the blood of the Lamb, their testimony, and by not loving themselves.

It was a happy occasion. Satan no longer controlled the dead. With the blood of Christ, God cleansed the dead who had kept covenant relationship with him and had not loved their lives unto death. These are the Old Testament saints who were cleansed when Christ ascended to heaven. This cleansing signified the beginning of salvation, strength, the kingdom of God and the rule of Christ.

The Dragon Persecutes the Woman

Vv. 12-17 The heavens rejoice, but the earth suffers because of Satan's fall. First, he persecuted **the woman** and then **the remnant of her seed.** She escaped Satan's wrath because God hid her for three and a half years.

The woman who brought the savior into the world represents the righteous of the nation of Israel. The righteous Jews living during the personal ministry of Jesus aligned themselves with Him. When Jesus ascended, they were left to become the church in Jerusalem. Satan desired to persecute and destroy the woman, so he cast a flood out of his mouth to wash away everything in its path. By directing his flood at the nation of Israel, he expected to destroy the Jewish church, but God intervened providing the Jewish church with a way of escape (cf.Matt.24:15-18; Lk.21:20). Failing in his efforts, Satan turned his fury upon the church following the war. **The Earthly Apocalypse** deals with the development of these conflicts.

Home Exercise
Chapter 12

TRUE OR FALSE:

1. _____ The great red dragon is identified as Satan.
2. _____ He is pictured casting fire out of his mouth.
3. _____ Those who overcame did so by animal blood.
4. _____ The glorious woman gave birth to a boy baby.
5. _____ She fled into the wilderness for seven years.
6. _____ Her child ascended to the throne of God.
7. _____ There was war in heaven between Michael and his angels and the devil and his angels.
8. _____ Satan deceived Michael, overcame him and cast him into the earth.
9. _____ Satan cast a flood of water after the woman.
10. _____ The kingdom came when Christ brought salvation into the world through his blood.

MATCHING:

1. _____ man child
2. _____ Satan
3. _____ the woman
4. _____ crown
5. _____ great eagle
6. _____ 1260 days
7. _____ earth
8. _____ remnant
9. _____ 7 heads
10. _____ wilderness
11. _____ dragon's tail

a. keep the commandments
b. the woman's place
c. swallowed flood
d. ⅓ of stars
e. rule all nations
f. 10 horns & 7 crowns
g. accuser of brethren
h. 12 stars
i. two wings
j. clothed with the sun
k. time, times, ½ time

MULTIPLE CHOICE:

1. The woman with child represents (Israel; Mary; Elizabeth).
2. The man child represents (Moses; Elijah; Jesus).
3. The dragon tried to (exalt; devour; adopt) the man child.
4. In the wilderness the woman was (nourished; starved; swallowed up).
5. The Woman and the Dragon are called (wonderful; wonders; adversaries).

Lesson 17

Chapter 13

The Emerging of Satan's Helpers

Chapter 12 develops the spiritual conflict between Christ and Satan up to the Roman-Jewish war and thereafter as it erupted into open conflict through the many persecutions that followed. It continues today. The chapters following develop the specific forces employed by Satan in attacking the church. God used the same instruments in directing His wrath against Israel.

The Sea Beast

Vv. 1-8 With the dragon standing on the seashore, a beast with seven heads, ten horns and ten crowns rose out of the sea. Upon his heads was the name of blasphemy. He was like a leopard with feet like a bear and a mouth like a lion. The dragon gave him power, a seat and  great authority. One of the heads was wounded to death but the deadly wound was healed and the world wondered after him, worshiping him and Satan, who gave him his power. He was permitted to speak blasphemies for 42 months against God, his tabernacle, and them that dwelt in heaven, and he made war with the saints and overcame them. This beast had authority over all nations, and everyone worshiped him except Christians.

Satan introduced his helpers in the conflict. His first helper was a beast out of the sea. He was from far and symbolizes the rise of Rome as a world power. He had seven heads symbolizing his complete power and authority. In 17:9, the heads are identified as seven mountains and kings, i.e., the first seven kings of Rome (cf.page 10). Upon the heads was the name of blasphemy which probably identifies the Roman practice of idolizing the Emperors as gods (cf.Jn.10:33). He had ten crowned horns which are **"ten kings, which have received no kingdom as yet; but receive power as kings one hour with the beast"** (17:12). These were the tributary kings who served the Roman Empire.

The empire operated with the swiftness and smoothness of a leopard, the strength of a bear, and the terrifying power of a lion. He received his power, seat and authority from Satan who deceived the nations (20:3,8; Lk.4:5-6). God does not deceive the nations to do wickedly (Hab.1:12-17). Through righteousness He exalts a nation (Prov.14:34). Oppression, war, hatred, strife, murder, etc., are works of Satan. Rome, and all other dominating empires, are built and sustained by Satanic influences. God at times has used these deceived nations to accomplish His purpose (cf.Isa.10:5-7; Dan.8:23-25; Rev.11:15), but the wickedness of the nation was the result of Satan's influence.

One of the heads had a fatal wound which had healed. There are two possible explanations: (1) Julius Caesar, the architect and first ruler of the empire, was murdered in 44 B.C. in a plot to kill the empire.[25] The wound was healed and the empire survived 13 years later when Augustus became emperor. (2) Nero, who instigated the first Roman persecution against Christians, committed suicide throwing the empire into turmoil and raising hopes the beastly empire had died but, after 18 months of confusion, Vespasian claimed the throne returning the rule of the empire. #1 seems most probable. After Augustus solidified his position as emperor, the world beat a path to Rome's door.

The beast developed a mouth which spoke blasphemies against God, his tabernacle (church), and those dwelling in heaven, and he made war with the saints (cf.Dan.11:35-36). No emperor fits this picture like Nero. Thinking himself a god, he poured his fury upon Christians.

Eventually, all under Roman rule worshiped the empire and her emperors except Christians. Their refusal resulted in the many Roman persecutions of the church which followed.

The Patience and Faith of Saints

Vv. 9-10 Saints suffered at the hands of the beast but God gave comfort by promising that those who persecute are destined to the same fate they assign others. Nero died by a sword in his own hand.

---

[25] Ogden, Arthur M., *The Avenging of the Apostles and Prophets* (Ogden Publications, 1985) pages 76-77.

The Earth Beast

Vv. 11-18 A second helper appeared; a beast out of the earth with two horns speaking as a dragon. He exercised the power of the sea beast and caused men to worship the sea beast. He deceived men by pseudo-miracles into making an image of the sea beast for worship and caused all who would not bow to be killed. He demanded that all men receive the mark of the beast, either in their right hand or forehead, before they could buy or sell.

This helper was later called **the false prophet** (16:13; 19:20). He had horns, but not as many or as powerful as the sea beast. He spoke as a dragon symbolizing his relationship to Satan. He served the sea beast who in turn served the dragon. Since the sea beast represents Rome, the earth beast represents the religions which served Rome's purposes. Caesar's images were erected in all the pagan temples and the worshipers of the gods were directed to worship the empire and the emperors.

Pagan priests were able to perform tricks that resembled miracles and deceive the people into thinking they were of the gods (cf.Acts 8:9-10). Thus deceived, the people served the empire. The **mark of the beast** was an invisible sign of submission to the **empire** as the seal upon the foreheads of God's servants is an invisible sign of submission to Him. The empire's servants were marked in the forehead to symbolize submission with the mind, or in the right hand to symbolize forced submission. To buy or sell, they must have the mark, the name of the beast or the number of his name. This means they had to serve the empire willingly or as a slave, be a Roman citizen, or a member of Caesar's administration. The number of this beast was 666 and is widely recognized as identifying Nero Caesar. For discussion of the number of the beast see page 10.

Home Exercise
Chapter 13

MATCH BEAST TO CHARACTERISTICS:

A. Beast out of Sea	B. Beast out of Earth
_____ two horns	_____ seven heads
_____ deadly wound	_____ voice of dragon
_____ great authority	_____ like a lamb
_____ lion's mouth	_____ miracles
_____ gave image life	_____ caused a mark
_____ feet of a bear	_____ fire from heaven
_____ miracles	_____ ten horns
_____ resembled leopard	_____ caused worship
_____ name of blasphemy	_____ power from dragon

TRUE OR FALSE:

1. _____ The sea beast was a helper of Satan.
2. _____ The number **666** symbolizes **satanic influence.**
3. _____ The sea beast made war with the saints.
4. _____ You can have the mark of the sea beast today.
5. _____ The earth beast was good because he was able to get people to worship God.
6. _____ Christians would not worship the sea beast.
7. _____ The earth beast performed real miracles.
8. _____ The sea beast ruled over many nations.
9. _____ The earth beast served the sea beast who in turn served the dragon.
10. _____ The world wondered after the sea beast.

ANSWER THE QUESTIONS:

1. What comfort is there in the patience and faith of saints? ___
   _____

2. How long was the sea beast permitted to blaspheme? _____
   _____ Who, what, and how did he blaspheme? _____
   _____

3. Explain what you think is meant by the receiving of a mark in your forehead, and/or right hand. _____
   _____

4. How would you apply the mark of the beast to our present society? _____

Lesson 18

Chapter 14

God's Righteous Judgments

Vv. 1-5 John saw the Lamb standing on mount Zion with the 144,000, sealed in their foreheads, and he heard a voice from heaven like that of many waters, great thunder and harpers harping. They were singing a new song before God which no man could learn but themselves. They were redeemed, purified and without fault, being the first-fruits unto God and the Lamb, and they followed the Lamb wherever He went.

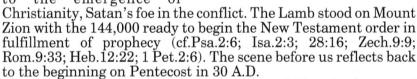

Our attention now turns to the emergence of Christianity, Satan's foe in the conflict. The Lamb stood on Mount Zion with the 144,000 ready to begin the New Testament order in fulfillment of prophecy (cf.Psa.2:6; Isa.2:3; 28:16; Zech.9:9; Rom.9:33; Heb.12:22; 1 Pet.2:6). The scene before us reflects back to the beginning on Pentecost in 30 A.D.

The 144,000 were singing a new song which only they could learn. Earlier we identified them as the redeemed of the nation of Israel who lived during the Mosaic age (cf. page 47). Only they could learn this song because only they of all the world ever stood in this position. They died in faith without the remission of their sins (cf.Heb.11:12,39-40) but, through the blood of Christ, they obtained eternal redemption (Heb.9:15; 12:23). They were perfect before God because their earthly lives ended before their cleansing. Having been cleansed they stood before God without the slightest imperfection.

The Everlasting Gospel Is Preached

Vv. 6-7 John watched as an angel flew through the midst of heaven with the everlasting gospel to preach to all the nations. With a loud voice he proclaimed, *"Fear God, and give glory to him; for the hour of his judgment is come: and worship him that made heaven, and*

earth, and the sea, and the fountains of waters."

The scene is Pentecost, 30 A.D. when the gospel was first preached under authority of the great commission to every nation (Matt.28:18-20; Col.1:23). Its message called upon men to fear God (cf.Eccl.12:13-14), prepare for the judgment, and worship the creator (cf.Acts 24:25).

Babylon's Fall Proclaimed

V. 8 A second angel followed proclaiming **the fall of Babylon.**

The first messenger proclaimed the gospel to all nations. This one announced the fall of Babylon. The message is secondary to the first. It is the message of doom upon Babylon. She was not identified here, but we have identified her as Jerusalem (cf. pages 12-13).

Empire and Emperor Worshipers Warned

Vv. 9-11 A third angel appeared, warning of the consequences of worshiping the beast and his image, and receiving his mark. Those guilty would drink of the wine of God's wrath and be tormented with fire and brimstone in the presence of the angels and the Lamb, without rest, day and night for ever and ever.

To worship the beast and his image was to worship the empire and the emperors. Temples throughout the empire were built for this purpose. Also, the pagan temples within the empire added the busts of emperors among the gods for the people to worship. This practice dated back to the time of Julius Caesar. Near the close of the first century, or the beginning of the second, Emperor worship began to be demanded by the state. Christians who refused were put to death.

The Patience of Saints

Vv. 12-13 A voice from heaven proclaimed the patience of saints, i.e., those who keep the commandments of God and the faith of Jesus. ***"Blessed are the dead which die in the Lord from henceforth: Yea, saith the Spirit, that they may rest from their labors; and their works do follow them."***

The demands of the Lord and the state are sometimes in conflict. Believing the Lord and keeping His commandments may lead to death but we should not fear. God cares for those who believe and obey him.

The Reaping of the Good Harvest

Vv. 14-16 John beheld one like the son of man, wearing a golden crown and having a sharp sickle in his hand, sitting upon a white cloud. An angel out of the temple cried unto him to thrust in his sickle and reap, and the earth was reaped.

Dark clouds symbolize storms and white clouds peace. This is a peaceful reaping. The first fruits of the new harvest were ready. The seed sown on Pentecost were ready for harvest a generation later. Stephen was the first recorded reaping of the New Age. Others followed both as martyrs and saints who were faithful until death. Perhaps the overcomers of 7:9 and 14 are included in this reaping.

The Reaping of the Vine of the Earth

Vv. 17-20 Another angel came out of the temple in heaven with a sharp sickle. He was told by an angel from the altar, who had power over fire, to gather the clusters of the vine of the earth because her grapes were fully ripe. The grapes were gathered, cast into the great winepress of God's wrath and trodden without the city. Much blood was extracted. (See front cover.)

The vine of the earth was the nation of Israel (cf.Psa.80:8-19; Isa.5:1-7). Her grapes being ripe means **her iniquity was complete.** When Israel's sins were complete, the time for God's vengeance came. Gathered in Jerusalem, a walled city, in April of 70 A.D., the Jews were suddenly surrounded by the Roman armies and treated to a barrage of arrows, darts, stones and swords until the last drop of blood was extracted. This is a fitting description of the destruction of Jerusalem.

Home Exercise
Chapter 14

FILL IN THE BLANKS:

1. The 144,000 stood with the _____ on mount _____ having been _____ in their foreheads.
2. Their voice sounded like _____ _____, _____ _____, and _____ harping with their _____.
3. The 144,000 sang a _____ _____ before the throne of God which _____ _____ could learn but themselves.
4. The 144,000 were _____ from the earth, were not _____ with _____, _____ the Lamb wherever he went, and were the _____ unto God.
5. _____ are the _____ which die in the _____, that they may _____ from their _____.

MATCHING:

1. _____ thrust in thy sickle	a. Babylon
2. _____ gather the clusters	b. the winepress
3. _____ without fault	c. no rest
4. _____ preach	d. faith of Jesus
5. _____ the great city	e. grapes are fully ripe
6. _____ one like son of man	f. Isaiah 5:1-7
7. _____ trodden without city	g. the everlasting gospel
8. _____ commandments of God	h. blood
9. _____ day or night	i. reap
10. _____ the vine of earth	j. upon a white cloud
11. _____ horse's bridles	k. 144,000

MULTIPLE CHOICE:

1. Babylon made the nations drink of the wine of her (vineyard; winepress; fornication).
2. God's winepress produced (wine; blood; cider).
3. The angel from the altar had authority over (fire; reaping; the winepress).
4. The 144,000 were all (men; women; virgins).
5. One might be guilty of worshiping the beast by worshiping his (picture; bust; statue).

Lesson 19

Chapter 15

The Seven Last Plagues

In **The Heavenly Apocalypse** (4-11), the stage was set with the introduction of the destructive forces by which Israel would be destroyed (ch.6). This was followed by the beginning of the New Testament order and the spread of the gospel (ch.7). The fall of the nation followed the opening of the seventh seal which signaled the beginning of the end.

The Earthly Apocalypse (12-20) follows a like pattern. The stage was set in chapters 12-13. Gathering the vine of the earth for the winepress of God's wrath followed (14:14-20), signaling the fall of the nation. As the opening of the seventh seal (8:1) was followed by the seven trumpeting angels, so the winepress scene is followed by the seven angels with the seven last plagues. These pour God's wrath upon the nation to the bitter end.

The Angels of the Last Plagues Introduced

V. 1 John saw another great and marvelous sign in heaven; seven angels with the seven last plagues filled with the wrath of God.

A **sign** signifies helpful information, and this sign pictures the fullness of God's wrath being poured out. God had threatened Israel with these plagues if they were disobedient to His laws and commandments (cf.Lev.26:15-32; Deut.28:58-59; 29:22-24). He had poured out His wrath by these plagues upon Israel often and abundantly (cf.Isa.42:24-25). John observed God preparing to pour out His wrath upon Israel to the fullest and for the final time. The fullness of God's wrath was poured out in 70 A.D.

The Testimony of Jewish Christians

Vv. 2-4 John saw what appeared to be a sea of glass mingled with fire. Standing on the glassy sea with the harps of God were those who had overcome the beast, his image, his mark and the number of his name. They were singing the songs of Moses, and of the Lamb, saying, **"Great and marvelous are thy works, Lord**

God Almighty; just and true are thy ways, thou King of
saints. Who shall not fear thee, O Lord, and glorify thy
name? for thou only art holy: for all nations shall come and
worship before thee; for thy judgments are made manifest."

The saints rejoiced before the throne of God standing on the
sea of glass. The sea was mingled with fire to symbolize the
refining fires of trials which purify the faith of saints, as gold is
purified, in order to make them acceptable to God (cf.1 Cor.3:9-15;
1 Pet.1:6-7).

Who are these saints? Remember the reaping scenes of chapter
14? The first scene was the reaping of the good harvest; the
righteous of the earth (14:14-16). The first fruits of the harvest
were Jewish Christians. We see them now praising God. They sing
the **song of Moses** (cf.Ex.15:1-19), and the **song of the Lamb.**
Only Israelites can sing the song of Moses, and only Christians can
sing the song of the Lamb. These are Jewish Christians who
refused to submit to the demands of the Roman empire and its
citizens. Their harps symbolize their victory as dead saints
(cf.14:2). They had been faithful unto death.

The heavens ring with the joy of their song and God was
praised for His great and marvelous works. It was a song of victory,
joy, and salvation in which God was praised for his **righteous
acts**. In their dead state, they understood that everything God had
said and done was **true and just.** Their salvation and God's
punishment of Israel were true and just acts of God.

The Angels of the Last Plagues Appear

Vv. 5-8 Afterward, John saw the temple of the tabernacle of the
testimony open in heaven. Out of it came the seven angels with the
seven last plagues, clothed in pure and white linen and with golden
girdles upon their breasts. One of the **living things** gave each a
vial, or bowl, full of God's wrath. The temple was then filled with
smoke from God's glory and power. No one was able to enter into
the temple till the plagues were fulfilled.

The temple of the tabernacle of the testimony in heaven is the
shrine of the dwelling place of God. The angels came from God's
dwelling place showing that this outpouring of wrath was of God.
They were clothed in priestly garments associating them with the
Son of God, our High Priest. The full and final judgment upon
Israel was committed to Christ (cf.Matt.24:30,36; Jn.5:27), and
these seven angels represent His couriers of wrath against Israel.

When the bowls of wrath were distributed to the angels, the
temple was filled with smoke. This happened also when Moses
finished building the tabernacle (Ex.40:34-38), and when Solomon
finished the temple (2 Chron.5:11-14; 1 Kings 8:10-11).

Symbolically, it is filled again, and means that God's new spiritual house was completed. As pointed out previously, the destruction of Jerusalem was a sign of the fulfillment of all that God had promised.

For a period of time no one was able to enter the temple until the seven plagues were fulfilled. The passage probably refers to the period of three and a half years of inactivity on the part of the Christians who left Jerusalem in late 66 A.D. (cf.Lk.21:20-21). The woman, which became the church in Jerusalem, fled to the wilderness for three and a half years (12:6,14). Being inactive, conversions were not made and no one was able to enter until the judgments were complete.

Home Exercise
Chapter 15

MATCHING:

1. ___ Plagues	11. ___ Great	a. ways
2. ___ White	12. ___ King	b. God
3. ___ Glass	13. ___ Glory of God	c. sea
4. ___ Lamb	14. ___ Angels	d. smoke
5. ___ Temple	15. ___ Pure	e. seven
6. ___ Just	16. ___ Moses	f. works
7. ___ Marvelous	17. ___ True	g. song
8. ___ Vials	18. ___ Almighty	h. sign
9. ___ Holy	19. ___ Girdles	i. linen
10. ___ Fire	20. ___ Judgments	j. golden

QUESTIONS:

1. Define **plague:** _____
   What is the significance of the **last plagues?** _____
   _____

2. List the things the victorious saints overcame? _____
   _____

3. In brief terms, what was the Song of Moses about (cf.Ex.
   15:1-5)? _____
   _____

4. What is the Song of the Lamb about? _____
   _____

5. Why should we fear the Lord and glorify His name? _____
   _____

TRUE AND FALSE:

1. _____ Verse 2 proves we can have mechanical instruments
   of music in church worship.
2. _____ When the temple of the tabernacle of testimony was
   opened, people flooded in.
3. _____ An angel gave the seven bowls of wrath to the four
   beasts.
4. _____ God's glory and power were so powerful they caught
   the temple on fire.
5. _____ God can pour out His wrath and still be just and true
   in all of His ways.

Lesson 20

Chapter 16

The Bowls of Wrath

V. 1 A great voice out of the temple commanded the seven angels to pour their bowls upon the earth.

Since New Testament saints suffered for the cause of truth (cf.6:11) and the new order was completely established, it was time for the consummation of all things previously determined to be carried out (cf.Dan.9:27; 11:36).

The First Bowl

V. 2 The first angel poured his bowl upon the earth and a noisome and grievous sore fell upon those who had the mark of the beast and who worshiped his image.

Since we are applying the Apocalypse to the desolation of Israel, our application must be directed toward Palestine as the place upon **earth** (land) under consideration. A plague of the worst kind was directed toward those in sympathy toward Rome. Josephus relates how the fury of the rebellious Jews turned upon those among them who sympathized with Rome.[26]

The Second Bowl

V. 3 The second angel poured his bowl upon the sea and it became as the blood of a dead man killing all in it.

This bowl, like the second trumpet, affected the **sea** (cf.page 51). The messages are identical. All sea battles were disastrous for the Jews.

---

[26] Josephus, *Wars*, 2,13,6; 2,14,9.

The Third Bowl

Vv. 4-6 The third angel poured his bowl upon the rivers and fountains of waters and they became blood. Then the angel of waters declared, *"Thou art righteous, O Lord, ...because thou hast judged thus. For they have shed the blood of saints and prophets, and thou hast given them blood to drink; for they are worthy."*

Like the third trumpet, this bowl affected the **rivers** and **fountains of waters.** The rivers and fountains of waters are the streams of power and influence which permeated the nation. They were filled with blood symbolizing the amount of blood shed among those in power. God was then praised for giving blood to drink to those who were responsible for the blood of the saints and **prophets** (cf.page 13).

The Fourth Bowl

Vv. 8-9 The fourth angel poured his bowl upon the sun and men were scorched with great heat and blasphemed the name of God and repented not.

This bowl affected the **sun** differently than the fourth trumpet. Men were scorched with great heat, probably symbolizing destruction by fire during the war.[27] For this God was blamed and blasphemed,[28] by people who refused to repent (cf.page 55).

The Fifth Bowl

Vv. 10-11 The fifth angel poured his bowl upon the seat of the beast, filling his kingdom with darkness and causing severe pain. They too blasphemed God because of their suffering and repented not.

The beast represents the **Roman Empire,** and the seat of the beast, **Rome.** The kingdom was filled with darkness symbolizing confusion and uncertainty. God was blamed for it all. This is a vivid picture of the conditions that developed when Nero died. Josephus tells how the empire was thrown into turmoil with civil wars and strife in different parts of the empire.[29]

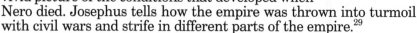

---

[27] Josephus, *Wars,* 3,4,1; 4,8,1; 4,9,9; 5,6,2; 6,5,5; 6,6,3.

[28] Josephus, *Wars,* 4,6,3; 6,2,3-5.

[29] Josephus, *Wars,* Preface,3; 7,4,2-3.

The Sixth Bowl

Vv. 12-16 The sixth bowl was poured upon Euphrates whose waters were dried up preparing the way of the kings of the East. Three unclean spirits came forth from the dragon, the beast and the false prophet. By these, the kings of the earth were gathered for the battle of the great day of God Almighty. Assurance was given those who watched and kept their garments, as the armies were gathered in Armageddon.

Like the sixth trumpet, this bowl was poured upon Euphrates. The purpose was to symbolically show that the way was prepared for the Parthians, Rome's most feared enemy, to come and join the Jews in the conflict, but they did not come. Satan, Rome, and the false religions of the empire called the nations together for this great battle. To the Romans, their fight against the Jews was a battle against God but, to God, it was His judgment against Israel.

In the midst of preparation for battle, Christians were warned to watch and keep their garments lest they also suffer in the conflict for lack of preparedness.

The place of gathering for this army was **Armageddon.** It means **mountain of Megeddo** and identifies Mount Carmel to which Megeddo was attached. It was in this region that Titus gathered his armies for the assault on Jerusalem in 70 A.D.[30]

The Seventh Bowl

Vv. 17-21 The seventh bowl was poured into the air and a voice out of the temple declared, *"It is done."* Great demonstrations of God's power followed. The great city was divided into three parts. Babylon was remembered. Islands and mountains were removed and God was blasphemed because of the greatness of the plague.

God poured His wrath upon Israel and, in doing so, destroyed Babylon (Jerusalem). She was divided into three parts both politically and geographically.[31] The rest of the language describes the chaos following Jerusalem's destruction.

---

[30] Ogden, *The Avenging of the Apostles and Prophets,* pages 319-320.

[31] *Ibid.,* page 322.

Home Exercise
Chapter 16

MATCH TO THE CORRECT BOWL(S) OF WRATH: 1-7

1. _____ Euphrates
2. _____ Earth
3. _____ It is done
4. _____ miracles
5. _____ thunder
6. _____ blasphemy
7. _____ blood
8. _____ Armageddon
9. _____ Babylon
10. _____ seat of beast
11. _____ eastern kings
12. _____ mark of beast

13. _____ great heat
14. _____ The great city
15. _____ great hail
16. _____ islands flee
17. _____ rivers
18. _____ sea
19. _____ sun
20. _____ darkness
21. _____ a sore
22. _____ fire
23. _____ sores
24. _____ frogs

QUESTIONS:

1. Why was God said to be righteous in verse 5? _____

_____

2. Why were those punished worthy to drink blood? _____

_____

3. How may we prevent exposing our spiritual nakedness to others? _____

_____

4. What is the meaning of the earthquake as a symbol? _____

_____

MULTIPLE CHOICE:

1. Three unclean (frogs; kings; spirits) came out of the mouths of the dragon, beast and false prophet.
2. The place where the armies were gathered was (Euphrates; Armageddon; Babylon).
3. Hail fell out of heaven that weighed (30; 70; 100) pounds.
4. The unclean spirits were able to gather the nations to battle by using (force; wine; miracles).
5. The people blasphemed God because of (pain; hail; earthquakes).

Lesson 21
Chapter 17

Babylon the Great

Chapter 14 closed with the winepress of God's wrath being trod outside the city. Chapters 15 and 16 took a closer look at the development of the Roman-Jewish war as God's promised judgment upon Israel and Jerusalem. In each case, **Babylon** was remembered and judged (14:8; 16:19). No attempt was made to identify her. Now an angel makes her identity known. Many believe Babylon symbolizes Rome but, as observed, her characteristics only fit Jerusalem.

Babylon's Characteristics

Vv. 1-6 One of the seven angels with the bowls of wrath showed John the judgment upon the great whore that sat upon many waters. She had committed fornication with the kings of the earth and made the inhabitants of the earth drunk with the wine of her fornication. John was in the spirit when he saw her. She was sitting upon the scarlet colored beast which had seven heads and ten horns, full of names of blasphemy. She was decked with gold, precious stones and pearls, and had a golden cup in her hand full of abominations and filthiness from her fornications. Upon her head was written, **"MYSTERY, BABYLON THE GREAT, THE MOTHER OF HARLOTS AND ABOMINATIONS OF THE EARTH,"** and she was drunk with the blood of the saints and the martyrs of Jesus. John wondered with great admiration when he saw her.

Who is this harlot? She sat upon **many waters** symbolizing **peoples, multitudes, nations, and tongues** (17:15). This characterized Rome, but it was also true of Jerusalem (cf.Acts 2:5-11). Jerusalem was the capital of the Jews scattered among the nations.

The inhabitants and kings of the earth committed fornication with Babylon (i.e., they engaged in all kinds of intercourse together). Israel was married to God and should have leaned upon Him but, instead, they turned to the kings of the earth for help. (Read the prophets.) In this she committed what God called **fornication** and became a harlot (cf. Hosea). Ezekiel said of her that she was *"old in adulteries"* (Ezek.23:43). Israel was accused of fornication and adultery from the time of the judges (Jud.2:17; 8:27,33; 1 Chron.5:25). These charges were directed at Jerusalem once she became the capital of Israel (Isa.1:21; Jer.2:20; Ezek.6:9; Mal.2:11). The whoredom and abominations of no other city compare to those of **Jerusalem** in God's sight.

The mystery of the great harlot must be spiritually discerned because Jerusalem was a spiritual city. The name upon her forehead indicates a mysterious identity. Jerusalem had been portrayed with the harlot's forehead for centuries (Jer.3:1-3). She was decked with all manner of precious things (cf.Jer.4:30). Jerusalem was probably the richest city in the world at the time of her destruction.

Babylon was drunk with the blood of the saints and the martyrs of Jesus. Some think these two groups are the same, but suppose John intended to include Old Testament saints. If so, the blood of saints identifies Old Testament saints and the martyrs of Jesus New Testament saints. Only Jerusalem fits the picture.

Babylon's Relationship to the Sea Beast

Vv. 7-13 The angel tells John of the mystery of the woman and the beast carrying her. The beast was, was not, and then ascended out of the abyss to go to perdition. All, except Christians, would wonder about this beast. The seven heads on which the woman sat were seven mountains and kings of which five were fallen, one was, and the other was not yet come. When he came, he would continue a short space. The beast that was, and is not, and yet is was of the seven, though he was the eighth, and would go to perdition. The ten horns were ten kings who had not received a kingdom yet, but had received power with the beast one hour. With one mind they gave their power and strength to the beast.

Babylon was carried by the beast which represents the Roman empire. This is significant. If the beast represents the empire (cf. pages 70-71), the harlot cannot be Rome. Rome was the beast. This city was not the beast or any part of the beast.

We previously discussed the identity of the seven heads which were seven kings (cf. page 10). Nero was the sixth. Upon his death, three emperors assumed the throne (Galba, Otho, and Vitellius) but, over a period of 18 months, each was quickly disposed of. None of them really ruled the empire. Finally, Vespasian, the seventh, took the throne and ruled the empire. Vespasian then sent his son Titus, who was of the seven, to carry out the war against the Jews until Jerusalem was destroyed (perdition). He is said to be **the beast that was and is not and yet is.** The beast was Rome, but the beast could only be seen in the presence of the Roman army. Vespasian withdrew the army from the war to claim the throne for himself. The beast that **was** left the scene and **was not.** It **returned** under the leadership of Titus to complete the war. Upon the death of Vespasian, Titus came to the throne as the eighth emperor of Rome.

The ten horns represent kings who had no kingdom of their own. These were kings like the Herods who governed the provinces. With one mind they gave their power and strength to the empire.

Babylon's Unmistakable Identity

Vv. 13-18 John was told that the beast with the ten horns would make war with the Lamb who would overcome them with His called, chosen and faithful because He is Lord and King. The horns would also hate the whore, make her desolate and naked, eat her flesh and burn her with fire. They would hate the whore because God put it in their hearts to fulfill His will in giving their kingdoms to the beast until God's words be fulfilled. The woman was that great city which reigned over the kings of the earth.

The war against Christians was pictured by John as a future event. The Lamb with His followers win this war. The primary function of the horns was to carry out God's will by giving their power and strength to the beast in destroying Babylon. She would be completely wiped out. None of this could apply to Rome, the eternal city, for Rome has never been destroyed. Babylon was the great city which reigned (lit. hath a kingdom) over (above) the kings of the earth. Rome through her kings ruled over the kings of earth but Jerusalem, **as a city,** had a **rule** that was above that of kings.

Home Exercise
Chapter 17

QUESTIONS:

1. What made the inhabitants of the earth drunk? _____

2. With what was the harlot intoxicated? _____

3. What do the **waters** symbolize? _____

4. What do the **seven heads** of the beast symbolize? _____

5. What do the **ten horns** symbolize? _____

6. Who gave their power and strength to the beast? _____

7. What was going to happen to the harlot? _____

8. What other passages in Revelation mention Babylon? _____

9. Describe Babylon? _____
_____

MATCHING:

1. _____ Reigns over the kings of earth   a. Lord of lords
2. _____ Ascends out of the bottomless pit b. the great whore
3. _____ Mystery, Babylon the Great   c. the scarlet beast
4. _____ King of kings   d. with the Lamb
5. _____ Full of abominations and filth   e. hate the whore
6. _____ The judgment was upon   f. the golden cup
7. _____ The ten horns   g. Mother of harlots
8. _____ The called, chosen and faithful   h. the great city

TRUE OR FALSE:

1. _____ The harlot and beast symbolize the same things.
2. _____ This is the same beast described in 13:1-7.
3. _____ This beast killed the witnesses in 11:7.
4. _____ Rome is identified as a harlot in the Bible.
5. _____ The ten kings were not a part of the beast.
6. _____ Rome killed most early Christian martyrs.
7. _____ Rome was responsible for the prophet's deaths.
8. _____ The beast's war with the Lamb was future.
9. _____ Jerusalem is **the great city** in the Revelation.
10. _____ John was shown the judgment upon Babylon by one of
         the seven angels with the bowls of wrath.

Lesson 22

Chapter 18

The Fall of Babylon

Reasons for Babylon's Fall

Vv. 1-3 John saw another angel coming down from heaven with great power and the earth was illuminated with his glory. He was shouting, *"Babylon the great is fallen, is fallen, and is become the habitation of devils, and the hold of every foul spirit, and a cage of every unclean and hateful bird. For all nations have drunk of the wine of the wrath of her fornication, and the kings of earth have committed fornication with her, and the merchants of earth are waxed rich through the abundance of her delicacies."*

The message was the same as the one proclaimed in 14:8. The messenger is closely associated with the Son of God. His message did not mean Jerusalem was already destroyed when John saw this, but that the time for it had come. There would be no further delay (cf.10:6). The transgressions of the nation were full (cf.1 Thess.2:14-16). John's picture described historical reality.[32]

A Call to the Saints to Leave Babylon

Vv. 4-5 John then heard another voice saying, *"Come out of her my people, that ye be not partakers of her sins, and that ye receive not of her plagues. For her sins have reached unto heaven, and God hath remembered her iniquities."*

This voice reflects perfectly the plea of Jesus for His disciples to leave Jerusalem when they saw the signs giving evidence of her approaching destruction (cf.Matt.24:15-18; Mk.13:14-16; Lk.21:20-21). History records that the disciples heeded this call and fled Judea for a place in the mountains called Pella.

The Call for Double Punishment

Vv. 6-8 The voice continued, calling for Babylon to be rewarded double according to her works because she glorified herself, and

---

[32] Ogden, *The Avenging of the Apostles and Prophets,* page 236.

lived deliciously. She boasted saying, *"I sit a queen, and am no widow, and shall see no sorrow."* Therefore, her plagues would come in one day (death, mourning and famine), and she would be utterly burned with fire as judgment from God.

The sins of Babylon reached heaven where God remembered all of her iniquities. A double reward of punishment was deserved and called for. Israel had rejected both, the Law and Prophets, and Jesus Christ. In addition, Jerusalem was held responsible for the deaths of both the prophets and apostles. God held her accountable **for all the righteous blood shed upon the earth.**

Boasting of her married relationship to her King (Hos.2:1-13), Israel could never conceive of God leaving her (cf.Mic.3:11-12). Josephus relates how the Jews continued to think this way as the city was being destroyed in 70 A.D.[33]

Lamentations over Babylon's Destruction

Vv. 9-19   John next observed the kings of the earth who committed fornication with Babylon lamenting over her destruction. This was followed by the merchants of earth weeping and mourning over her because this great center of trade was being closed to them. The shipmasters and mariners also cried when they saw the smoke of Babylon's burning.

Jerusalem was a great city of commerce due to the constant influx of tourists who came each year to worship God. Several times a year they came by the millions. Today, cities fight over conventions which sometimes bring a few thousand people and millions of dollars. Jerusalem, however, through the power of her position as the center of Jewish worship, constantly drew people, money and trade. Her destruction saddened kings because of the loss of revenues, and it saddened the merchants because of the loss of business.

It is interesting to note the first ten items listed in verse 13. All of these were used in Jewish temple worship services under the Law of Moses (cf.Ex.30; 1 Chron.9:27-29).

The Heavens, Apostles, and Prophets Rejoice

V. 20 *"Rejoice over her, thou heaven, and ye holy apostles and prophets; for God hath avenged you on her."*
In the midst of great lamentation there was room for rejoicing. The heavens, saints (NIV and other translations), the holy apostles and prophets could rejoice because their blood was finally avenged. God promised it, the prophets and saints cried for it (6:10), and the

---

[33] Josephus, *Wars*, 5,11,2; 5,2,1.

deaths of the apostles and saints demanded it. When it came, they
could rejoice.

The Desolation of Babylon

Vv. 21-23 John saw a mighty angel take a large stone and cast it
into the sea. This was to show that Babylon was to be violently
overthrown never to exist again. Musicians, craftsmen, the candle,
the bridegroom and his bride would no more be in this city
because, by her sorceries, she deceived the nations who destroyed
her. In her was found **the blood of prophets, saints, and all
that were slain upon earth.**

Since the city was to be wiped out never to exist again, all that
made it happy and joyous would be gone forever. Jerusalem, the
city of God under the Law, would never exist again. Today, there
is a city on the same spot called Jerusalem, but it is not the city
God destroyed. Without the temple, that city cannot exist.

She was destroyed because the blood of God's servants was
shed in her. Jesus identified **Jerusalem** as the city in which the
blood of God's servants was shed (cf. pages 12-13).

Home Exercise
Chapter 18

TRUE OR FALSE:

1. _____ The blood of prophets, saints and all that were slain upon the earth was found in Babylon.
2. _____ Merchants were happy to see Babylon destroyed.
3. _____ God called for His people to leave Babylon.
4. _____ Babylon's sins deserved double punishment.
5. _____ Babylon's ruin was only the loss of prestige.
6. _____ Babylon was a wealthy city.
7. _____ Ten items in verse 13 were used in the Temple.
8. _____ Babylon was expected to return to prominence.
9. _____ Evil people filled Babylon before her burning.
10. _____ God avenged the saints, apostles and prophets.

MATCHING:

1. _____ Riches came to naught   a. reached to heaven
2. _____ Kings of the earth   b. I sit a queen
3. _____ Voice of bridegroom   c. is strong
4. _____ Babylon's sins   d. the great city
5. _____ Became rich through her   e. found no more
6. _____ I shall see no sorrow   f. heard no more
7. _____ Cried at her burning   g. rejoice over her
8. _____ Nations were deceived   h. in one hour
9. _____ The Lord who judges   i. merchants of earth
10. _____ Dainty & goodly things   j. by her sorceries
11. _____ Decked with gold   k. lived deliciously
12. _____ Saints, apostles, prophets   l. Merchant marines

FILL IN THE BLANKS:

1. With _____ Babylon was _____ _____ and _____ no more.
2. All nations _____ of the _____ of the _____ of her _____, and the _____ of the earth committed _____ with her, and the _____ of earth became _____ through her _____.
3. God's people were told to _____ _____ _____ _____ lest they be _____ of her sins and receive her _____.
4. List the things no more to be heard in her: _____, _____, _____, _____, _____, _____, _____.

Lesson 23
Chapter 19

Victory of Christ over All Foes

The Earthly Apocalypse has centered upon the conflict between Christ and Satan. This led Satan to direct his fury against Israel in an attempt to destroy the woman which became **the church.** Satan fails in his efforts to destroy the woman (12:14-16). In the process, God used Satan's instruments to accomplish His own will in bringing the nation of Israel to an end by destroying Jerusalem (17:16-17). Now, our attention turns to a consideration of the conflict that was yet to develop between Christ and Satan (12:17; 13:7-8; 17:14). We are permitted only a general view, yet we see it developing from its inception unto the end of time.

Victory Celebration over Babylon's Fall

Vv. 1-6 John heard a great voice of many people in heaven praising God with **alleluias** and attributing to Him **salvation, glory, honor, and power.** They were praising Him because He had demonstrated His **true and righteous judgments** in judging Babylon and avenging the blood of His servants at her hand. The **four living things** and the **twenty-four elders** also joined the heavenly chorus. A voice then was heard saying, *"Praise our God, all ye his servants, and ye that fear him, small and great."* The voice of a great multitude followed saying, *"Alleluia: for the Lord God omnipotent reigneth."*

This is the victory celebration of saints over Babylon's destruction. It is the same celebration pictured in 11:15-18 following the destruction of the city were our Lord was crucified. God righteously judged Israel and Jerusalem and **avenged the blood of his servants at her hand.** Truly, from their standpoint, it was an occasion of rejoicing (cf.18:20).

Celebration over the Lamb's Marriage

Vv. 7-10 Praise continued as the multitude changed the reason for their praise of God. They rejoiced because **the marriage of the**

lamb came and his wife made herself ready. She was granted the privilege to be arrayed in fine linen, clean and white. John was then instructed to write, *"Blessed are they which are called unto the marriage supper of the Lamb."* When John saw all of this, he fell at the feet of the angel guiding the vision to worship him, but was refrained.

While the desolation of Israel and the destruction of Jerusalem was cause for great rejoicing by the martyred saints, the salvation portrayed by the marriage of the Lamb is of greater significance. The Lamb's wife is **new Jerusalem** (Rev.21:2,10) which on earth is **the church** (Eph.5:22-32; 1 Cor.11:1-2). When one obeys the gospel of Christ (Mk.16:15-16), he is added to the church (Acts 2:38-39,41,47) and married to Christ (Rom.7:4). By this process we are washed from our sins in the blood of Christ (Rev.1:5; cf.Acts 22:16) and begin wearing our white robes (Rev.7:14). Our robes are kept white by the blood of Christ (cf.1 Jn.1:7) and our righteousness (1 Jn.3:3,7). The clean and white fine linen **is the righteousness of saints** (Rev.19:8).

The fourth beatitude promises great blessedness to those called to the marriage supper. Like our **wedding reception,** the marriage supper followed the wedding celebrating the marriage. It would sometimes last for days, even weeks, and in some cases longer. By comparison, through the gospel (2 Thess.2:14), all men are called to come and partake of the great feast of good things provided by the God of heaven (Eph.1:3). This feast was made possible by the marriage of the Lamb to His bride, new Jerusalem (21:2,10; cf.Matt.22:1-10).

The King of Kings and His Armies

Vv. 11-16 Heaven opened and John saw a white horse whose rider was called Faithful and True and who judged and made war in righteousness. His eyes were as flames of fire. He had many crowns on his head and a name written which no one knew but himself. He was clothed with a garment dipped in blood and his name was called **The Word of God.** His armies followed Him clothed in fine linen.
Out of his mouth extended a sharp sword with which to smite the nations. He ruled them with a rod of iron. He tread the winepress of God's wrath. On his vesture and thigh was written, **KING OF KINGS, AND LORD OF LORDS.**

We now see the Lamb, the Son of God, our King of kings and Lord of lords in a different light. He is in complete control. Babylon is gone. The blood of her destruction spots the garment of Him who carried out God's wrath against her. So, our picture portrays our King following the destruction of Jerusalem. He and His saints are ready to fight against all foes.

The Defeat of the Sea and Earth Beasts

Vv. 17-21 Next, John saw an angel calling the vultures together for the supper of God in which a feast of kings, captains, men, and horses would be served. John saw **the beast** and **the kings** of earth gather to make war against the rider of the white horse and his armies. The beast and the **false prophet** were taken and cast into the lake of fire and brimstone. Those left were slain with the sword of him that sat upon the white horse. The fowls enjoyed a great feast.

This battle is the one foretold earlier in the Apocalypse (12:17; 13:7-8; 17:14). It follows the destruction of Babylon (Jerusalem) and portrays the war that developed between the Roman Empire, Pagan religion and the Church. It began early in the second century,[34] and continued into the reign of Constantine to 313 A.D. When the smoke cleared after the persecutions ended, the Roman Empire and the Pagan religions that served her were gone. The Lamb and His armies continue to this day fighting every foe and winning every battle.

---

[34] The ground work for Roman's persecution of Christians was laid during the reign of Emperor Domitian, though evidence of any persecution from the history of the times is lacking. The first evidence of a state persecution against Christians comes during the reign of Trajan (98-117 AD).

Home Exercise
Chapter 19

MATCHING:

1. _____ Called to supper of lamb	a.	Faithful and True
2. _____ Worshiped God	b.	judgments
3. _____ On white horse	c.	The Lamb's army
4. _____ Flame of fire	d.	corrupted earth
5. _____ Many crowns	e.	in one hour
6. _____ Smite the nations	f.	Lake of fire
7. _____ The great whore	g.	Testimony of Jesus
8. _____ Vesture dipped in blood	h.	The fine linen
9. _____ Beast and False prophet	i.	Blessed
10. _____ Clothed in fine linen	j.	Treading winepress
11. _____ Righteousness of saints	k.	eyes
12. _____ The spirit of prophecy	l.	head
13. _____ True and righteous	m.	Lamb's wife
14. _____ Made ready	n.	sharp sword

DO THE FOLLOWING EXERCISE:

1. Write out the **beatitude** of this chapter: _____
_____

2. List the names of the rider of the white horse:
_____, _____,
_____, _____.

MULTIPLE CHOICE:

1. The rider of the white horse judged and made war (in the sun; in righteousness; in heaven).
2. The (bride; Lamb; armies) were clothed in white.
3. The rider of the white horse ruled with an iron (thumb; staff; rod).
4. He had a (friend; name; disease) which no one knew but himself.
5. Out of his mouth came a (viper; fire; sword).

TRUE OR FALSE:

1. _____ The marriage of the Lamb will take place during the great tribulation period.
2. _____ God avenged His servants when Babylon burned.
3. _____ The rider of the white horse got blood on his vesture when He was crucified.
4. _____ Babylon was to be rebuilt.
5. _____ The supper of the great God proves it is scriptural to have a kitchen in the church building.

Lesson 24

Chapter 20

Unto the End of the World

The Binding of Satan

Vv. 1-3 An angel descended from heaven with the key to the abyss and a great chain in his hand. He laid hold upon the dragon (Satan), bound him for a thousand years, cast him into the abyss, and shut him up. He put a seal upon him that he should deceive the nations no more until the thousand years were fulfilled.

Satan's helpers, the Roman Empire and the religions that served the Empire, were defeated and destroyed at the close of chapter 19. The binding of Satan followed in an effort to curtail his power. He was bound that he should **deceive the nations no more** until after 1000 years. He would then be loosed for a season to deceive the nations again (cf.20:8).

Three things are of significance when discussing the binding of Satan: (1) His binding should not to be considered a complete imprisonment causing cessation of **all** his powers. He was bound only that he should **deceive the nations no more.** (2) His binding followed the destruction of his helpers which means that any count of time must begin **after** the fall of Rome and the Pagan religions that served Rome. (3) By all reasonable counts, the period of 1000 years has passed.

The Reign of the Saints

Vv. 4-6 John saw thrones and those sitting upon them had been given judgment. He saw the souls of those who were beheaded for the witness of Jesus and the word of God. They had not worshiped the beast or his image, and had not received the mark of the beast. They lived and reigned with Christ a thousand years. The rest of the dead did not live again until the thousand years were finished. This is the first resurrection. Those who have a part in it will not be hurt of the second death and will be priests of God and Christ and reign with him the 1000 years.

The question must be raised; **what happened to all of those who lost their lives in the conflict between Christ and Satan previously described?** John had already said they would rest from their labors (cf.14:13). Now, he pictures them **living and reigning** with Christ. For as long as Satan is bound they continue to reign. Who are they? Martyred saints who lost their lives because they refused to bow to the state and its supported religions. They were dead, but continued to live and reign with Christ because they had a part in the first resurrection. Because of this, the second death, which is eternity in the lake of fire and brimstone (20:14), has no power over them.

The first resurrection has been explained a number of ways. The Premillennial view is the most popular. They teach that Christ will resurrect the righteous. This, they say, is the first resurrection. Then, after a seven year period of tribulation, Jesus will return to earth to reign on earth in Jerusalem for 1000 years. Others teach that the 1st resurrection is the resurrection from baptism to walk in newness of life (Rom.6:4). Still others teach it is the resurrection of the Christian cause. None of the above harmonize with the context of this chapter.

We must remember that John saw the souls of those who were physically dead. These souls lived and reigned with Christ even after death. The rest of the dead did not live again until after the 1000 years. Why not? Because, they were spiritually dead as well as physically dead which means they continued to be separated from God. Those who are spiritually alive continue to live even though they are physically dead (cf.Jn.11:25-26; 2 Cor.5:8-9; Phil.1:23). The scene described here is the same as that pictured by Jesus in Luke 16:19-31. The only difference is Jesus described the **hadean** realm as it existed under the **Law** while John described it under **Christ.**

The Loosing of Satan

Vv. 7-10 When the 1000 years expired, Satan was loosed to deceive the nations again. He gathers them from the four quarters of earth to battle. They came up on the breadth of the earth and compass the camp of the saints, the beloved city. Fire came down from God out of heaven and devoured them. The devil was then taken and cast into the lake of fire and brimstone with the beast and false prophet to be tormented day and night for ever and ever.

Apparently this is intended to be a forecast of what will happen before the end comes. Satan will be permitted to gather his forces from all quarters of the earth and compass the saints. Whether this means there will be a severe persecution of the saints before the end comes, or simply that the saints will be caught in the middle by Satan's tactics, we cannot tell. All we know is that God will end the matter with fire from heaven which will destroy the nations. Satan and his works will be brought to an end.

The Final Judgment

Vv. 11-15 Finally, John saw the great white throne and him that sat upon it. Heaven and earth fled away and there was found no more place for them. All of the dead stood before God and the books, and the book of life, were opened. The dead were judged by the things written in the books according to their works. Death and hell which delivered up the dead in them and all who were not found in the book of life were cast into the lake of fire and brimstone. This is the second death.

John viewed the end of all things. Heaven and earth passed away (2 Pet.3:10-12). The judgment began (Matt.25:31-32). The dead were raised (Jn.5:28-30) and judged according to God's word (Jn.12:48; Rom.2:16). Those who were not found in the book of life were cast into the lake of fire along with **death** and **hades** which had served their purpose. The final judgment is concluded. Eternity begins.

Home Exercise
Chapter 20

TRUE OR FALSE:

1. _____ Satan was bound so he could not do anything.
2. _____ The beheaded saints of 20:4 were Christians.
3. _____ Christ will reign on earth 1000 years.
4. _____ Those having a part in the second death will have had no part in the first resurrection.
5. _____ Satan will be loosed for the battle of Armageddon.
6. _____ Fire from heaven devoured the beloved city.
7. _____ The devil will be cast into the lake of fire.
8. _____ Gog and Magog symbolize the U. S. and Russia.
9. _____ Those buried at sea will escape the judgment.
10. _____ The second death is for those who have had **a near death experience.**

QUESTIONS:

1. What benefits are promised those who have a part in the first resurrection? _____
_____

2. Considering your answer to the preceding question, could the first resurrection be:
   a. Resurrection from baptism?   Yes   No
   b. The resurrection of a cause?   Yes   No
   c. Resurrection into Paradise?   Yes   No

3. In your opinion, who or what is the **beloved city?** _____
_____

4. What are the books by which the dead were judged? _____
_____

MATCHING:

1. _____ Every man was judged   a. Devil and Satan
2. _____ The devil   b. The lake of fire
3. _____ Stand before God   c. in hand of angel
4. _____ Bound a 1000 years   d. Satan was bound
5. _____ That old serpent   e. nations
6. _____ Heaven and earth fled   f. the dragon
7. _____ The second death   g. Great white throne
8. _____ Deceive nations no more   h. Tormented for ever
9. _____ Gog and Magog   i. According to works
10. _____ Key to abyss   j. all of the dead

Lesson 25

Chapter 21

The Glorious City Described

Introduction

The principle subject of the Apocalypse has been discussed and the things shortly to come to pass revealed. Ancient Jerusalem, the city of God, has been pictured in destruction. Now our attention turns to the emergence of **new** Jerusalem, God's new city, which replaced **old** Jerusalem.

Since **The Earthly Apocalypse** ended with the judgment and the punishment of the wicked, it is only natural for us to expect the vision to continue with the righteous being rewarded in heaven. However, in Revelation we have come to understand that John often viewed what had already been seen. This is the nature of this section of Revelation. It presents what has already been revealed in the previous sections even though it was not always called the new Jerusalem.

The new Jerusalem presented by John is a composite of all of God's Old Testament promises to build a new and different Jerusalem. Many texts contribute information concerning this glorious city envisioned by God. Isaiah 65-66 portray God's wrath being poured upon Israel as punishment for their sins followed by the creation of a new heaven and earth and a new, different Jerusalem. The promises revealed by Isaiah are many and have their fulfillment under Christ and the New Testament order.[35]

The new Jerusalem is clearly seen in the writings of the New Testament. Paul said, *"But Jerusalem which is above is free, which is the mother of us all"* (Gal.4:26). The Hebrew writer said, *"Ye are come unto mount Sion, and unto the city of the living God, the heavenly Jerusalem, ...to the general assembly and church of the firstborn...and to the spirits of just men made perfect"* (Heb.12:22-23). New Jerusalem is composed of the church and the spirits of just men made perfect.

---

[35] See Homer Hailey's excellent *Commentary on Isaiah*. Hailey observes that the promises of a new Jerusalem are fulfilled in Christ.

The perfected spirits of just men are Old Testament saints who were cleansed with the blood of Christ when the atonement for sin was offered and accepted (cf.12:10-11). The church is married to Christ (Eph.5:25-32). As sinners obey the gospel, they are added to the church (Acts 2:47) and married to Christ (Rom.7:4). So, God's new Jerusalem is a spiritual city composed of **all** who have been redeemed with the blood of Christ. John's picture of **new Jerusalem** is the same as that envisioned elsewhere in the Old and New Testaments.

The New Heaven and New Earth

V. 1 John observed a new heaven and earth without seas as the first heaven and earth passed away.

A new physical universe is not envisioned. John is simply seeing a new heaven and earth through changes. Reorganization makes new. This is the use made of the expression in the Old and New Testaments (Isa.65:17; 66:22; 2 Pet.3:13). We have observed these changes in our studies. The **new heaven** was created by the appearance of the Lamb at God's right hand where He assumed His position as King of kings (cf. chapters 4-5). The **new earth** was created at the same time through the atoning blood of Jesus Christ (cf.12:10-11). The first heaven and earth passed away, i.e., the law was taken out of the way and nailed to the cross removing the barriers between the nations so all can be acceptable to God.

New Jerusalem Introduced

V. 2 John saw the holy city, new Jerusalem, coming down from God out of heaven, prepared as a bride adorned for her husband.

New Jerusalem descended from heaven adorned as a bride. In this attire, we observed her before. The victorious saints who rejoiced over the destruction of Babylon 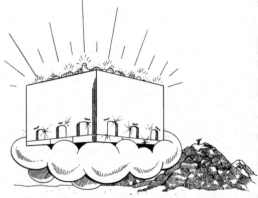 the Great praised God that the marriage of the Lamb took place and His wife made herself ready (19:7-9). At the time of Jerusalem's destruction, the marriage had already taken place. In the scene before us, John saw her coming out of heaven prepared as a bride for her husband. John was viewing the beginning of the new order; not the end. The Old Testament prophets foretold that when the Gentiles were brought into covenant relationship with God, He would be married to this spiritual Jerusalem (Isa.49:18; 61:10; 62:4-5; Hos.2:16-23). Jesus likewise prophetically portrayed His marriage to this bride (Matt.22:1-14; 25:1-13), and the New Testament writers pictured the marriage as having taken place (Rom.7:4; 2 Cor.11:2; Eph.5:22-23). New Jerusalem is the bride of Christ, the Lamb's wife. On earth, she is represented by the church of Christ. In heaven she is represented by the redeemed saints of all ages.

The Old Testament Prophets Fulfilled

Vv. 3-5 Next, John heard a great voice from heaven declaring that the tabernacle of God is with men. God will dwell with them. They will be His people and He will be their God. He will wipe away all their tears. There will be no more death, sorrow, crying or pain because the former things passed away. God said, *"Behold, I make all things new."* Then, He commissioned John to write, because His words were faithful and true.

It is difficult for us to understand these things in association with the present age, yet these were things promised by God to be characteristic of this age (cf.Isa.21:4; 25:7-8; 65:12-17). Jesus taught the same things during His personal ministry (cf.Lk.6:21; Jn.5:24; 6:50-51; 8:51; 11:25-26; 16:20-22). If we can understand what Jesus was teaching in the above passages, we can understand their reality in relationship to **new Jerusalem.**

The former things associated with old Jerusalem passed away. They were nailed to the cross (Col.2:14). Now, God has made **all things new** (cf.Isa.42:9). We have a **new covenant** (Heb.9:15), and a **new church** (Eph.2:15). We become **new creatures** (2 Cor.5:17), possess **new life** (Rom.6:3-4), inhabit **new Jerusalem** (Rev.21:2), wear a **new name** (Isa.62:2; Acts 11:26; Rev.22:4), and sing a **new song** (Rev.5:9). It is a present reality because God's words are **faithful and true.**

Promised Rewards and Punishments

Vv. 6-8 God, who is the Alpha and Omega, the beginning and the end, proclaims, *"It is done."* He then invites those athirst to drink of the water of life, promising a father and son relationship and an inheritance of all things to those who overcome. At the same time He promised the lake of fire and brimstone to the fearful, unbelieving, abominable, murderers, sorcerers, idolaters, and all liars.

The proclamation that *"it is done"* means that the things associated with new Jerusalem were already a reality when John saw the Apocalypse. It being accomplished, God promised access for those athirst to the water of life (cf.22:17).

Overcomers benefit from the blessings afforded in new Jerusalem. The overcomer is the one who gains the victory over Satan and sin. He is rendered pure and free from sin because defilement is not permitted in the new city (21:27; 22:15; cf.Isa.35:8-9). He inherits all things because as a Christian he becomes an heir of God with the promise of a full inheritance (Rom.8:16-17; Gal.3:26-29; 4:7). The lake of fire, which is the second death, is reserved for those who do not overcome.

The Physical Features of the New City

V. 9 One of the seven angels with the seven last plagues invited John to take a closer look at the bride, the Lamb's wife.

The seven angels of the last plagues poured out the wrath of God upon the nation of Israel and when the seventh angel emptied his bowl, Babylon (Jerusalem) was remembered (16:19). One of the seven angels then showed John the identification of Babylon (17:1). The appearance of one of these seven angels to show John new Jerusalem reveals a correlation between Babylon and new Jerusalem. The relationship is simple. Babylon symbolized Jerusalem which was replaced by **new** Jerusalem.

Vv. 10-21 From a high mountain John saw the city descending out of heaven from God. The glory of God lighted the city like a jasper. It was a city four-square, approximately 1400 miles in every direction. Its walls were 210 feet thick with twelve gates of pearl, an angel at each gate, and the names of the tribes of Israel on the gates. It had twelve foundations with the names of the apostles upon them. The city was of pure gold with a street of gold.

The city sustained a continuing relationship with God as it descended out of heaven to earth. It is a marvelous city to behold. It is large enough to hold the worlds redeemed and the walls thick enough to protect them. It can be entered from any side.

Vv. 22-27 There was no man-made temple there. God and the Lamb are the temple and light of it. The nations of the saved walk in its light and the kings of earth bring their glory and honor into it. The gates are never closed, and nothing can enter that is defiled, works abomination, or tells lies. Only those whose names are in the book of life can enter.

One of the first things one would see approaching old Jerusalem was the temple, but God and the Lamb are the temple of new Jerusalem and dwell in her midst. It is a spiritual city relying upon spiritual light (2 Cor.5:7). Only the saved walk there (cf.Acts 2:47; 1 Jn.1:7). Entrance is always available through gates that never close (cf.Acts 16:30-34). Sin and iniquity are not permitted. Sin is left outside the gates as sinners repent and obey the gospel (cf.22:14). Those who enter are those whose names are written in the Lamb's book of life (cf.Acts 2:41,47; Phil.4:3; Heb.12:22-24).

This is a beautiful city, but it is not a city that pertains to the physical. It is a spiritual city and must be spiritually discerned. Attempts to conceive of this city as physical miss the point.

Home Exercise
Chapter 21

MATCH CHARACTERISTICS OF NEW JERUSALEM:

1. _____ New Jerusalem   a. each gate
2. _____ A great wall   b. the street of it
3. _____ Twelve gates   c. saved of the nations
4. _____ Twelve foundations   d. approx. 1400 miles
5. _____ The temple of it   e. of jasper
6. _____ Pure gold   f. death, sorrow, crying
7. _____ The light of it   g. came down from heaven
8. _____ One pearl   h. God and the Lamb
9. _____ 12,000 furlongs   i. Holy Jerusalem
10. _____ The Lamb's wife   j. 12 tribes of Israel
11. _____ Walk in its light   k. the Lamb
12. _____ The former things   l. the twelve apostles

COMPLETE THE FOLLOWING EXERCISE:

1. List those things characteristic of Old Jerusalem that would not be a part of New Jerusalem: _____

2. Who is not permitted in new Jerusalem? _____

   Who is permitted? _____

3. Determine the size of the new city and thickness of its walls: _____

4. List those things that were said to be **gold**: _____

TRUE OR FALSE:

1. _____ John saw new Jerusalem as a place in heaven.
2. _____ The new heaven and earth are a part of a newly created universe.
3. _____ Those who live and believe in Jesus will never die.
4. _____ Today, the bride of Christ is the church.
5. _____ Only the saved could walk in new Jerusalem.
6. _____ God does not dwell in the midst of the church.
7. _____ The sun shines brightly in new Jerusalem.
8. _____ It is always day in new Jerusalem.
9. _____ The fearful can find refuge in new Jerusalem.
10. _____ The gates of new Jerusalem are shut every night.

Lesson 26

Chapter 22

The Glorious City Continued

The Water of Life

V. 1 John observed a pure river as clear as crystal containing the water of life flowing from the throne of God and the Lamb.

God foretold the day when waters would flow permeating His new, different Jerusalem (cf.Isa.12:3; 30:25; 35:6-7; Ezek.47:1-2; Zech.14:8), and Jesus promised living waters during His ministry (Jn.4:14). He said, *"If any man thirst, let him come unto me, and drink. He that believeth on me, as the scripture hath said, out of his belly shall flow rivers of living water"* (Jn.7:37-38). John said he was speaking of the Holy Spirit (v.39). The function of the Holy Spirit was to reveal the word of God (Jn.14:16,26; 15:26; 16:13; Acts 2:1-4; 1 Cor.2:10-16). Faith comes by hearing the word of God (Rom.10:17). The **water of life** then is the satisfying, pure, **word of God** channeled to us through the Holy Spirit.

The Tree of Life

V. 2 In the midst of the street of the city and on each side of the river was the tree of life bearing fruit every month and its leaves healing the nations.

The purpose of the tree of life is to give life (cf.Gen.3:22). Originally, it was in the garden of Eden (Gen.2:9) but, when man sinned, he was driven from the garden and from access to the tree. Now, the tree reappears in new Jerusalem fulfilling God's promise to make new Jerusalem like Eden (cf.Isa.51:3).

We believe the **tree of life** symbolizes the **cross**. Everything mankind lost in Adam, including life and immortality, has been regained in Christ (1 Cor.15:22; Jn.6:51,54; 2 Tim.1:10; 1 Jn.5:11-16). The word **tree** (of life) is translated from **xulon**. It means, *"Wood, a piece of wood, anything made of wood."*[36] In every

---

[36] Vine, Vol. IV. page 153.

other usage in the New Testament where **xulon** is used, except Luke 23:31, it identifies the **cross** (cf.Acts 5:30; 10:39; 13:29; Gal.3:13; 1 Pet.2:24). Since the things lost through Adam are regained through the blood of the cross, it is only reasonable to assume that the **cross of Christ** is our tree of Life.

Unlike our fruit trees which bear fruit one month out of twelve, the **tree of life** bears fruit continually. The life giving fruits are always available to cleanse us from sin and give us life (cf.1 Jn.1:7). Since we often sin, we have constant need to partake of the benefits of its fruit.

While only those who keep God's commandments and enter new Jerusalem have a right to the tree of life (22:14), its leaves are for the healing of the nations. The benefits of the cross have fallen upon all nations and they have profited from it.

The Saints Reign

Vv. 3-5 There will be no more curse. The throne of God and the Lamb are in new Jerusalem, and His servants serve Him there. They see His face, and His name is in their foreheads. There is no night there, or need of the candle or the sun, because God gives them light. They reign for ever and ever.

There are no curses like those pronounced in Eden. Now, God forgives sins. God's servants serve Him in His new city. His face is seen there and His name is in the foreheads of His servants. They will reign forever.

A Summary Picture of New Jerusalem

The picture we see of new Jerusalem is enlightening. It enhances our understanding of the spiritual world of the righteous both living and dead. Both are citizens of this new city. The righteous dead are permanent citizens. They gained the ultimate victory as overcomers. They had a part in the first resurrection (20:4-6). They reign with Christ the thousand years. The righteous who live on earth are also citizens of new Jerusalem. They were viewed in their relationship to the seven churches as either being acceptable or unacceptable. If acceptable, they were overcomers and numbered among the inhabitants of new Jerusalem.

The Conclusion of the Book

The visions are over. The Revelation is complete. Only the concluding remarks remain. Jesus again personally addressed John in order to identify himself as the source of the Apocalypse. He also addressed John to invite *"whosoever will"* to come and be partakers of the blessings revealed in this marvelous book. Finally,

He warns those who tamper with the things revealed of the consequences of their actions.

Vv. 6-17   The last verses of the chapter affirm the quick appearance of the son of God. Those who keep the sayings of the book will have no problems.

John falls before the angel to worship him. John previously related this story in 19:10. The angel forbade John and directed him to worship God.

John was then instructed not to seal the prophecy because the time for its fulfillment was at hand. The Lord was coming quickly and His rewards would be with him.

A beatitude disclosing who had the right to enter the city and eat of the tree of life introduces the close of the book. Those who keep God's commandments are the only ones who can enter. Every other thing must stay outside.

The Lord then identifies himself as the offspring of David and the bright and morning star, and extends the invitation of the spirit and the bride. After warning of the consequences of adding to, or taking from, the words of the prophecy, John concludes with the promise of Jesus to come quickly. John gives his sanction to the promise.

Home Exercise
Chapter 22

QUESTIONS:

1. Cite the beatitude(s) in this chapter? _____

2. What happened to John when he saw this vision? _____

3. Do verse 18-19 apply to the whole Bible or just to Revelation? _____

4. Who is being invited by the Spirit and the Bride in 22:17? __

5. Who cannot enter new Jerusalem? _____

6. Do we have a need to eat of the tree of life today? If so, how often do we have this need? _____

FILL IN THE BLANKS:

1. A _____ _____ proceeded out of the _____ of God and the _____. It was _____ as _____ and contained the _____ of _____.

2. The _____ of _____ was in the _____ of the _____ and on both sides of the _____, and bear _____ fruits, one for each _____. The _____ of the tree were for the _____ of the nations. God removed the _____.

3. The _____ of God and the _____ would be in new Jerusalem. His _____ would serve him wearing _____ _____ in their _____.

4. John was told not _____ _____ the _____ of this book because _____ _____ _____ _____ _____.

TRUE OR FALSE:

1. _____ One may eat of the tree of life by faith only.
2. _____ Jesus is the root and offspring of David.
3. _____ Everything lost in Adam is regained in Christ.
4. _____ Jesus had already come in the destruction of Old Jerusalem when John saw this vision.
5. _____ In heaven, the inhabitants of hell will be invited to drink of the water of life freely.
6. _____ It would be thousands of years before the book of Revelation was fulfilled.

Lightning Source UK Ltd.
Milton Keynes UK
UKOW06f2201170817
307528UK00008B/258/P